Graham Foundation / MIT Press Series in
Contemporary Architectural Discourse

The Road That Is Not a Road

and the Open City, Ritoque, Chile

Graham Foundation for Advanced Study in the Fine Arts • Chicago, Illinois

The MIT Press • Cambridge, Massachusetts • London, England

Ann M. Pendleton-Jullian

The Road That Is Not a Road

and the Open City, Ritoque, Chile

This book was set in Bembo and Gill Sans by Graphic Composition, Inc. Printed and bound in the United States of America.

Library of Congress Cataloging-in-Publication Data
Pendleton-Jullian, Ann M.
  The road that is not a road and the Open City, Ritoque, Chile /
  Ann M. Pendleton-Jullian.
    p.   cm.
  Includes bibliographical references (p.   ) and index.
  ISBN 0-262-66099-7 (pbk. : alk. paper)
    1. City planning—Chile—Ritoque—History—20th century. 2. New towns—Chile. 3. City planning—Philosophy. 4. Universidad Católica de Valparaíso. Institute for Architecture. I. Title.
NA9053.N4P46   1996
711'.45'098255—dc20   96-17475
                                                             CIP

Contents

I first met Godofredo Iommi in the Hochschule für Gestaltung in Ulm: it
must have been in the fall or winter of 1958—the only time I was there—
preaching my belief in the historicity of perception and therefore of all de-
signing against what I considered then, and still do, the Ulm school's dumb
positivism in managerial disguise.

Even rebellious students there (who tended to follow a "vulgar" Marxism) were not much help. Iommi arrived—a diminutive, tubby, worried but
energy-charged poet of whose work I knew nothing as yet—and seemed so
different from both my colleagues and students that I took to him at once.
He appeared to me like a brilliant meteor against the gray flannel of the Ulm
backdrop. Tomas Maldonado—then director of the school and an old friend
of Iommi's who introduced us—sensed that we would have something in
common.

Iommi at once captured my sympathy by telling how, coming from
an anarchist family, he had taken seriously André Breton's declaration that the
true poetic act was to run into the street with a loaded pistol and shoot at random. Because he did not have the courage (or the will) to do this, he felt any
writing of his own would therefore be inauthentic—mere literature. A vis-
iting French writer shocked him out of his scruples by asking him if he knew
how the sublime Breton made a living (a question he had not considered),
and by telling Iommi that Breton did so by selling African art and the work
of painters he had befriended.

Breton was not the fiery angel, after all, but a smooth-talking art dealer. The revelation came as a salutary shock to the young Iommi. Though he may have been disappointed, personally, in Breton, he never lost faith in the validity of the poetic act. After some peregrinations, he moved to Chile. In Santiago he met Alberto Cruz who was already teaching architecture there. Soon after their meeting, in 1952, the new Jesuit rector of the Catholic University at Valparaíso appointed Cruz to run the school of architecture. While spending much of the next decade as a modern troubadour in Europe, especially in France, Iommi, Cruz, and their associates worked through the program of the school they wished to build in Valparaíso, which they brought into being in the seventies and eighties.

The Viña del Mar/Valparaíso school is unique in that it is autopoetic; it has quite literally built and planned itself, with each building seen as a poetic act. The way in which the ideas of the great literary and artistic movements of the inter-war period were developed and transformed, and the manner in which they flowered in the fertile Chilean soil, is Ann Pendleton-Jullian's story. Now that the way we train architects (and what we train them for) is under critical examination, this is a story that should be read by all involved in thinking about building.

Joseph Rykwert
April 1996

With the three Santiago architects who showed me around the noble city of Valparaíso and made me acquainted with its most tender aspects, I went to Viña del Mar where Alberto Cruz and Juan Purcell were waiting for us. We had a quick lunch together in a restaurant facing the Pacific. They knew my work and I knew theirs, having seen it a few days before at the Santiago Bienal in the publications of the Valparaíso Architectural School. Juan Purcell is now head of that school, and Alberto Cruz—who held that position until he retired—still has a role as an ideologist and inspirational figure. He believes that architecture should be born out of poetry: this much I knew, but I didn't imagine that this belief was literally applied with unrelenting consistency.

Strolling along the seafront before continuing our trip, they told me how their students approached a design by starting from a verse by Baudelaire, Rimbaud, or Neruda, from which they derived all the reasons for conceiving inhabitable spaces—which they then constructed directly, without mediation. They do not need a make-believe client, nor to invent programs, nor to refer to specific places because even the site has to be evoked by the poetic potential of the verse itself. Though it may also be true that having a given place in mind leads them to choose precisely that verse.

I asked why they chose such an elusive approach to the circumstances and means proper to architecture. Because, they answered, it is necessary to put forward radical alternatives to current architectural practice, which is subject to economic power and is therefore commercialized—in that it focuses on quantity and has a hypocritical attitude in regard to quality, providing ambiguous simulacra with the complicity of opportunistic or ignorant criticisms.

I must add, as I am afraid it is not clear from the above synthesis, that all this was expressed most quietly and gently, with the serene aloofness of people who are at peace with nature and all human beings. Without interrupting our conversation, we returned to our cars and headed for Ritoque through a landscape that increasingly turned into a vibrant sand desert. We were soon traveling on roads of beaten and stabilized sand with a herringbone-pattern surface of many layers of stubble—an ecological figure in tune with the land forms. Suddenly we saw among the dunes the students of the Faculty of Architecture of Valparaíso who, with their teachers, were erecting complex timber and iron structures roofed with metal, plywood, or plastic sheets and closed with glass, perspex, or opaque materials. Some of these structures were inhabited by young couples, teachers with families, or groups of students who had designed and built them and now were free to use them on the sole condition of taking care of their repair. And maintenance must be very painstaking and constant because the structures are very fragile and never reach a clear and definitive completion—in keeping with the hazy principle that underlies their design.

Each structure contains a lattice of fortuitously interpenetrating spaces with no visible junctions. Each space is at once kind and sullen, welcoming and off-putting: certainly unfit to house anything except forms of use totally different from the common and necessary ones of human beings leading a "normal" life.

"Do you consider yourselves a community?" I asked toward the end of the visit. They answered very calmly that they did.

"A utopian community?" I asked. "Yes, we think we are a utopian community."

So, what is the Ritoque utopia about? Well, it opens a series of questions that may be worth reflection and discussion—for example, that the primary concern of current building activity is financial, and so its products are mostly marketable commodities. Those who design and build as a profession engage in operations that must yield profits to their promoters, so they cannot evade the requirements of economic power and become inherently a party to making architecture a commodity. This complicity is consummated at a level of unawareness or hypocrisy, as in fact architects are always talking about philosophy or poetry, but most of their products are simply marketable. The extremes of this distortion are to be found in architectural education that, instead of preparing young architects to be disinterested inventors of spaces responding to the multiplicity of human needs, trains them to produce spaces as standardized as possible and thus more easily marketable. Ritoque's utopia, like every serious utopia, does not admit uncertain hypotheses—for example, that it is probably intrinsic to architecture to have to resolve apparently insoluble contradictions—and so aims at an absolute alternative, making use of all the hazards and certainties that its deliberate estrangement can offer.

Giancarlo De Carlo
Milan, November 1993

Preface

When I first visited Chile in the South American summer of 1987/1988, I was struck by the grandeur and nobility of its physical space, with how it is a grandeur and nobility that promotes and nurtures the intimate. In that same summer I inadvertently discovered the Open City in Ritoque, which is a site of confluence between this physical space of Chile and a mental space that extends beyond regional boundaries in both time and space yet, like the pigeon, always returns home. The Open City opened up to me the larger field of work of the Institute for Architecture of the Catholic University of Valparaíso in which pedagogical activity is speculative in nature and absolutely tied to a way of acting, doing, and making with a bias toward a kind of primitive glorification of the power of the imagination.

Because of this—because of the nature of the work that clearly prefers the endeavor over the result—it was important to me that the presentation of this work not fix itself in analysis but remain open to discussion. Therefore, what follows is intended neither as a critical opinion nor a historical or theoretical analysis but rather as a sympathetic presentation of the work and its mental site along with some of its more provocative issues.

I thank Alberto Cruz and Godofredo Iommi for their persistent hospitality and for the inspiration that is the Open City; Juan Purcell for his insight, assistance, and friendship; and the faculty of the Catholic University of Valparaíso for sharing their work; and I recognize in appreciation Guillaume Jullian de la Fuente, who introduced me to Chile, to Valparaíso, to the inside of Le Corbusier's atelier, and to the transgression of poetry into the field of architecture.

1 *Nos parece que la condición humana es poética, vale decir que por ella el hombre vive libremente y sin cesar en la vigilia y coraje de hacer un mundo*[1]

If one is heading north along the coast from Valparaíso, through Viña del Mar, toward Zapallar, and if one's eyes scan to the left traversing the region between horizon and coastline, past the rocky beaches, beyond the mouth of the Aconcagua River, the region between coast and horizon closes down and the region between coast and road expands to enclose low-lying dunes, some horses, and then a building whose gable end reaches up out of the sand to catch the wind in kinetic pantomime of an animal aroused from sleep.

From the road, this building is the most prominent of a group of constructions found among the dunes that comprise the Open City Amereida in Ritoque, Chile, which was conceived and built by the Faculty of Architecture of the Catholic University of Valparaíso—a group of architects, poets, artists, and engineers. The site is spacious and diverse, divided by the highway into two parts: the coastal dunes and the upper grass plateau. In the distance, within the mist of the sea, the dunes are crossed by a train that transports copper ore up the coast and ingots down. It moves in mechanical ambition across the far edge of the site. Parallel to the edge between land and sea and perpendicular to the movement of the waves that come and come and come without ever seeming to arrive on the beach, its purposeful movement naively mocks the destiny that is the sea's. The movements and sounds

1. *"It seems to us that the human condition is poetic, that is to say that for it man lives freely and without end in the vigil and courage to make a world."* Alberto Cruz, quoted by Vittorio di Girolamo, "Los Locos de Valparaíso," qué pasa (October 18, 1972): 49.

of the train convene with those of the sea to establish a first dialogue with the space of the site. In fact, the site is all movements, rhythms, and sounds: the sea, the sand, the wind, the light, and air, the motor traffic and train.

Two impressions form. A first impression: the site is land and space in one of its most transparent, ephemeral, and mutable states. A second impression: because of or in deference to these qualities of the land, the constructions on the site of the Open City are light. They attain a status of lightness. Consequently, there is an apparent lightness of physical impression onto the site.

Lightness because the way in which the constructions touch the ground does not demarcate territory of building through strong physical impact and authoritarian footprints but, instead, lets the land initiate the configuration of territory and space in both plan and section. Because of the movement of the sand by the wind and movement of the ground (earthquakes), building weights and volumes are supported by many points of contact distributed according to structural and spatial needs and intents. Volumes lifted off of the ground allow the natural migrations of the sand to continue uninterrupted, whereas those buildings that do make physical contact with the ground, whether it be shallow or profound physical contact, allow the physical forces of the site into their space. One gets the impression that if all the constructions were removed from the land, the land would not hold their memory.

Lightness, also, because the materiality of the constructions at the Open City is related to a type of construction that is artisanal, which remains attached to the physical process of building at the scale of the artisan and not the machine. It therefore reveals the hands of the builders and is a representation of human occupation of the site and not the mechanical domination and reconfiguration of the site. One senses the presence of raw nature and not manipulated landscape, of footsteps and not tire tracks.

And *status* of lightness because there are no apparent imposed formal ordering devices that regulate the development of the constructions. Instead each construction is attached to the space of the site through ideation and ideaphoria, which manifests itself as spatial strategies with spatial form and relationships. However, the forms and formal ordering devices do not come first and are not fixed but can transform as spatial specifics and tactics are developed. Because formal ordering of space is rendered through this mental activity and not through the (super)imposition of formal devices, physical centers and boundaries do not exist in any conventional way. Each building

has a center of gravity of sorts that remains unpunctual and difficult to locate with any precision because these centers are never formalized and because they migrate as constructions are added to or transformed. Occasionally groups of buildings, such as the Banquet Hospedería conglomerate, over time begin to reveal sets of centers of gravity: constellations, in that they produce, in addition to the individual centers of gravity, a center common to the set. Again, however, this point is not fixed but can migrate because it is a resultant, not a determinant, of construction activity. Often edges of constructions are even more illusive than their gravity centers just as the edges of the city have never been defined by walls or fences.

And *status* of lightness, also, because not only are physical centers and edges illusive but there is also a tendency for meaning to migrate and transform within single buildings and within the city as it has grown and matured over time: as new buildings are added to the site or existing buildings revised; as constructions are overtaken by the sands, winds, or other natural forces and left ruined or rebuilt and reoriented to the forces of the site.

La architectura como borde "que no es orilla ni límite, pues éstos separan uniendo, porque nos parece como un no más allá, un irreductible."[2]

From above on the upper grass plateau, perched high over the highway, one is able to survey much of the site of the Open City; and what is striking, beyond the constructions themselves, is the lack of hierarchy among the structures and the complete absence of any formally derived city plan. The notion of interior or exterior limits does not seem to exist at the city scale either. Instead the siting of the constructions seems to follow individual agendas related to the ideas at the interior of each. The roadways do not establish an order. There are no avenues and streets or axial/cross-axial relationships, no gridding or patterning. Instead the "roads" adapt themselves to the location of the structures, linking them to each other in point-to-point connections while navigating along the topographic irregularities of the terrain so as to create as little disturbance to the land as possible. Even the one "crossing" in the road seems to evaporate from the sand as you pass over it—more a mark of passage than a space. Public open spaces, the agoras, do not establish order or orientation but exist as independent entities laid out on the land in sites whose topographic forms facilitate the act of collecting and meeting or of introspective conversation with the natural movements of the site. Sequential development—functional, political, or religious in nature—

2.   *Architecture as edge "which is not border nor boundary, since these separate even as they unite, because it seems to us as a 'no further away', an irreducible." Ibid.*

does not establish order. Nor does building use or zoning. Physical centers and boundaries do not exist in any conventional urban way.

From above, it becomes immediately clear that instead of imposed ordering devices defining the characteristics of "city" and construction, the Open City's central posture is a suspension of plan and a consciously adopted ad-hocism that is generated by an attitude toward building in relationship to an attitude about the site.

The attitude toward building results in an ad-hocism that manifests a consistent material quality. Brick, concrete, and wood are the primary elements of construction, and the construction systems are semiartisanal. The building of the Open City has advanced only with funds coming from the Faculty of Architecture of the Catholic University of Valparaíso, and a significant part of the work was physically constructed by the faculty members and students. Scavenged building components, such as windows, are also built into the projects and sometimes inform initial design research. For these reasons—because these materials are inexpensive, common, familiar and because these construction systems are related to the physical process of building at the scale of the artisan—the materiality remains attached to the *process of building* as it reveals the hand of the builder.

Within the consistent materiality deriving from the attitude toward the building process and within the legibility of the building process itself, one notices two different strategies relative to the articulation of space and form. There are those buildings—such as the Music Room, the Palace, the hospedería at the entry, and the studios—that incorporate the building process into a set of design ideas. The construction begins with a certain notion of the whole, resulting in a structure that can be perceived with unity. And there are other buildings—such as the Banquet Hospedería, one of the first buildings to be built and one which is continually being worked on—in which the building process *becomes* the design process, resulting in structures that have an aggregative character. The members of the first species of structures are capable of being held in the memory as an image, however sketchy, whereas the members of the second species remain illusive and fragmentary.

The materiality and building attitude that link the discrete structures at the Open City provide an underlying theme that is, however, nonordered and nonformularized. The question then arises as to what it is that provides orientation within the city: how does one find one's orientation *within* the city and *to* the city where an adopted ad-hocism has replaced urban ordering devices? The relationship of the work to the site is one that is immediately

attached, without mediating elements, to the individual and his or her translation of the phenomena of this relationship. Therefore, it is through the site, both physically and mentally, often poetically and thematically, that orientation occurs. Light and sand act as two halves of the canvas on which the projects operate while the sea stands by as patron.

The relationship of the work to the site is one that (re-)searches for the essential and existential qualities of the natural environment through the discovery, interpretation, and translation of phenomena as they relate to the Chilean spirit. It is a relationship formed through the mind and mental activity, not through arbitrary associations or concerns of convenience. It insists on not converting the nature into a commodity or into "landscape" and therefore avoids domesticating the natural environment with mediating elements—especially the mediator of nostalgia, which subjugates nature to a romantic dementia. The relationship, instead, is an immediate one. The building does not occur in response to certain natural characteristics but allows the elemental qualities of the nature and its phenomena to generate the impulse for building and informally serve as components of an illusive thematic base structuring the development of the work.

Because it is about a profound relationship to the landscape as understood through its essential traits and existential qualities, it is not an attitude relative to specifics but to correspondences between things. Although there is a significant difference between the specific natural qualities found in the dunes versus in the highlands, this is less important than those qualities that are fundamental to both. In the highlands the site is in a spectacular position to view the sea. However, throughout the Open City the preferred attitude is one of turning one's back to the sea specifically because of its visual power and omnipresence. This seems paradoxical considering that the site was bought because of its proximity to the sea. However, in this way the buildings do not exist as servants to the sea but maintain a validity, in themselves and relative to the complexity of the natural space, to that which is obscure as well as transparent. Additionally, this positioning creates a condition in which a certain emotional distance is placed between the inhabitants and the sea to allow the sea's presence, not only its physical and visual reality, to open up the experience rather than close it down to be contained within the fixity of view. Stripped of its emotional haze, the sea as guardian, provider, storyteller, and so on is reattached to the individual mentally through one's imagination. Because the sea is a presence and not a commodity, there are no buildings built on the coastal border or on the beach.

The Pacific Ocean—its space and phenomena—is a presence that forms one of the two edges framing the Chilean space. The Andes Mountains are the other edge, and the site in Ritoque contains both edges, visually, within its space. And here, the sand—as the primordial state of the land, of the Andes Mountains—merges with the sea. As with the relationship to the sea, the work of the Open City recognizes the phenomena produced by the sand, its physical realities, and its potentiality of meaning. There is so much of it in varying degrees of stability and surface form. It moves. Maintained in a virgin state, this movement is uninhibited. The relationship of each work to this canvas is about the virginity and mutability of the sand: the way in which it accepts and erases imprints, its effect on the light of the sun and the sound of the ocean, its persistence in moving and migrating, the structural and spatial challenges and opportunities this poses. Even the roads must acknowledge the qualities of the virgin sand. They are therefore more pathways than roads and must search for the slope that will allow passage over them instead of clearing and moving the sand around, which will just move back unless it is constrained.

The relationship of the work to the sun goes beyond just the light and its random illumination but instead deals with the properties of light and shadow, or shades of grayness. It deals with light's transparency over the sand, its opacity and its ambient qualities. It exploits the sun's ability to trace out time through passage, thereby joining space to time. It involves itself with the sun's personification as the sun consummates its relationship with the sea upon arrival and with the mountains upon departure. And it celebrates the virginity of the night in which the clarity of the sky at this location, at the ocean's edge, makes the sun's absence more pronounced. The legibility of the movement of the stars is admired in the sun's absence and remembered in the sun's presence. The visual experience turns to the nocturnal as, in parallel, the mental experience discovers the world opened up by the nocturnal.

The orientation of oneself through the site as well as the lightness of physical impression on the site, the attitude toward the building process, the materiality, the interrelationships between these aspects, and the ad-hoc application of all the above create a type of work that has a striking similarity to the spontaneous and aggregative works of necessity found in the cities and the countryside of Chile, which are characterized by the term *vernacular.* What separates the works of the Open City from the vernacular, however, is a mental as well as physical link to the process and to the site. Whereas the vernacular architecture demonstrates a *way of building,* the work of the Open

City results in objects that demonstrate a *way of doing*. The vernacular relies on construction to make space that either conforms to or mitigates the difficulties of the natural context with regard to spatial needs. This construction relies on a certain intuitive process, but the editing of the intuitive process is regulated by the logistics of getting the thing built with what means one has. The other work—the work at the Open City—relies on a self-conscious way of acting and thinking that sponsors an intuitive process informed by spatial and poetic concerns. In this process the intuitive is edited by the process itself or by the logistics of the ideation, and space is the consequence. This way of acting and thinking about the building of space at the Open City has resulted in the informal development of a highly enigmatic and mutable thematic base that underlies the work, providing a possible unifying mental structure.

El acto engendra la forma; como el trazo que, al ser puesto a luz, orienta la normal indiferencia de las direcciones.[3]

Returning to this idea of an ad hocism that has replaced conventional urban ordering devices and to its relationship to an enigmatic thematic base: at the Open City it is an ad hocism in the precise definition of the word and one which manifests itself in the creation of a formal entity. Each structure, individually, employs the mental/thematic base and attitude toward the construction of space to the design process "for the particular end or purpose at hand and without reference to wider application or employment."[4] The thematic base does not create formal rules or formulas, nor does it imply the development of a consistent formal language, and the process is one that does not predetermine or in any way fix the material result. It is a mental construction that is not consciously derived, owing more to intuition that serves up recurring preoccupations, and it is constantly in a state of flux and revision.

Metaphorically related to the sand, which erases footprints, paths, and directions to present a clean surface upon which to walk or write, the mental attitude of the work at the Open City is one which prefers, instead of the stability of acquired knowledge, the adventure of an incessant "returning to not knowing" (*volver a no saber*). Just as the memory of the erased footsteps replaces the presence of the actual footsteps through the imagination's power to transform the real into the imaginary, the imagination transforms experience and knowledge to present it in a new form each time one is in face of the creative process. This incessant returning to not knowing is a very important

3.   *"The act engenders the form; like a pen stroke which, put to the light, orients the normal indifference of the directions." Ibid.*

4.   *See the definition of* ad hoc *in* Webster's Third New International Dictionary.

argument made by the Open City and could only result in a deference to the principle of ad hocism. It establishes a commitment to the belief in invention and reinvention.

Historically ad hoc urbanism leaves its trace on cities through the chronological legibility of the built city. One can usually read a decided area of first settlement, whether it is a center or an·edge, and then chronological movement away from that first area of settlement. The first area of settlement corresponds to a location in the site that fulfills programmatic needs of the city, whether those needs are related to subsistence, protection, commerce, or power. At the Open City, the first area of settlement occurred outside the city in time and space, within the pedagogical activity of the school. The proposition of city began there. On the site itself, a founding occurred that did not *locate* a physical beginning point but, instead, *discovered* a mental point of departure.

•

One of these (founding acts) consisted of going to the place during an entire day and night. Here they opened the sites. They ate in a forest and recited poems. When they tried to demarcate the central point, they sensed that the city did not have a point or axis which could give an order or hierarchy to its physical development. It was going to be 'unpunctual' and the siting of the works would derive solely from the poetical acts. They slept in the sand, and on the shore they dug a hole so that the sea could enter as in a fjord. They discovered the significance of the dunes, which are at the mercy of the winds, they are not earth, they are not sea, nor beach.[5]

•

They discovered the *volver a no saber* in the sand, which metaphorically relates to the mutability of the site and its phenomena.

Construction and constructions moved forward from this mental point of departure, inserting themselves into the site where the process of ideation determines they must be, not where plan or chronology arbitrarily places them. Chronology does not establish spatial order. There is a decided uniqueness to each construction on the site, and the constructions do not attempt to create spatial relationships between and among themselves. Dialogue is with the physical and mental space of the site and not with each other. Nor do they accept or set rules of formal or spatial logic. Within the material similarities and mental/thematic preoccupations, each building at the Open City exhibits its own beginning.

5. Enrique Browne, "Amereida: una experiencia arquitectónico—poética chilena," Summa no. 214 (July 1985): 76.

❷ *El 15 de junio de 1967 (fecha de la rebelión contra las autoridades de la UCV…) comenzó la tranformación de la Universidad proclamando su necesaria re-originación; palabra y acción fueron un gesto. Abierto el camino, el paso as lento.*[6]

The Open City was founded in 1970, but the experience from which it grew refers back to 1950 when the Chilean architect Alberto Cruz Covarrubias first met Godofredo Iommi, the Argentinean poet. Both men were thirty-three years old. Iommi was working in an advertising office in Santiago and Alberto Cruz was teaching in the Catholic University of Santiago. The meeting was significant because it established the beginning of a long and profound dialogue between poetry and architecture—between the word and space—and set the foundation for a pedagogical program of research based on this relationship.

Alberto Cruz studied architecture at the Catholic University of Santiago, which at that time was very much focused on the professional education of architects with a formal loyalty to the traditions of the École des Beaux-Arts. Between graduation and teaching, he traveled extensively through Europe and began a professional practice with two colleagues. As a teacher in the Catholic University's first design studio, he was known for his unconventional approaches. He would walk upon the tables as he lectured, responding to his students' questions with "¿Y tú qué piensas?"[7]

Godofredo Iommi was born in Buenos Aires and began his studies in economics, which he quickly left to devote himself to poetry. Just as an architect sincerely interested in the pursuit of modern architecture in the early nineteenth century turned his sights on Europe, and especially France, a poet wanting to establish a relationship with the avant-garde also looked to France and Europe. Ironically it was on one of his trips to Europe that Iommi initiated the discovery of his own continent as well. Just as he was to embark for Europe, Iommi's plans had to be cancelled because of the onset of World War II. As he was already in Rio de Janeiro, he decided to visit the interior of the Amazon with a group of Brazilian poets. This was the first of many trips into the South American continent and the beginning of an important poetic relationship between Europe/European culture and South America/Latin American culture. Upon eventually settling in Chile, Iommi married Ximena Amunategui, who had been connected with the Chilean poet Vincente Huidobro in Paris where she had been introduced to many poets and painters from the French and European avant-garde community.

6. "On the 15th of June, 1967 (date of the rebellion against the authorities of the Catholic University of Valparaíso …), the transformation of the University which proclaimed its necessary reorigination began; word and action would be one gesture. The road opened, the passage is slow." Cruz, "Los Locos de Valparaíso," 49.

7. "And you, what do you think?" Alberto Cruz, quoted by Vittorio di Girolamo, "Arquitectura UCV: Locos Por Fuera, Genios Por Dentro," qué pasa (October 18, 1972): 48.

Together, Alberto Cruz and Godofredo Iommi conceived of the idea of effecting a great switch, by removing architecture from its doctrine, buried in mathematics and formalisms, and centering it in the poetic word. Concurrently and conveniently in 1952, the Jesuit congregation took over the Catholic University of Valparaíso, and the new rector, Father González, decided to initiate a complete renovation of the school. He offered a post to Cruz, whose reputation for innovation ensured change. Knowing that a transformation of consequence could only be achieved by a comprehensive influence produced by a group of individuals dedicated to this task, Cruz agreed, stipulating that all or none would accept the appointment. "It served nothing to have a good professor. That which we had to have was a working group."[8] The group included eight: Alberto Cruz, Godofredo Iommi, Francisco Méndez, a painter and a group of young architects who were known for their open defiance of the conventional academic canon, Arturo Baeza, Jaime Bellalta, Fabio Cruz, Miguel Eyquem, José Vial. The Argentinean sculptor Claudio Girola joined them shortly afterward. The group began to teach and live together with their families in the Cerro Castillo, in a cluster of houses close to the university. They pooled their salaries and dispersed them according to the needs of each family as they engaged in research and debate not only within the pedagogic program but outside the university walls as well. The research engaged all aspects of living, and a common base was established in which no person had authority over another.

The force of the commitment of the transplanted Santiago group created a very strong impact on the architecture school's orientation and pedagogy. Almost immediately it was necessary to form, from the body of the school, an institute of architecture separate from the existing faculty and programs to provide an independence of structure for true and intense research. For this research, the institute focused on its studios as laboratories comprising architects, poets, painters, sculptors, and engineers. They rejected architecture as a profession because of the compromises necessary to form professionals, and no professor taught a student what he himself did not do. This created a very strong morality and an authentic university condition as a laboratory of thought.

The pedagogic program the institute presented was the following: to plant within the context of architecture the experience of working in group and the proposition of employing the poetic word as the foundation of an architectural polemic. And it insisted that the program of research engage the modern context.

8. "No servia nada tener un buen professor. Lo que había que tener era un grupo de trabajo." Godofredo Iommi, quoted by Margarita Serrano, "Godofredo Iommi. La Vida Peligrosa," Mundo no. 105 (August 1991): 11.

It is significant that the alliance to the modern was to be made through the poetic word and not directly through modern architectural precedent. The founders of the institute looked to the modern European, and especially French, poets who engaged modern culture in dialogue, not to the buildings of the modern European architects, which, in large part, approached modernity through the interrelationship of form and space to technology, and adopted a position of societal reform through the promises of technology and mass production.

Through poetry, the founders of the institute believed art that is true transcends its own materiality; true architecture, true sculpture, true poetry derives its sense from its ability to reveal the invisible of itself—interior truth not physical reality. Modern poetry questioned the relationship of these interior truths and values to the assumptions and values prescribed by the structures of modern culture, and it questioned its perceived imbalance of power between the two domains.

Tangentially, a brief comparison for discussion of context can be outlined here between the orientation and founding of the Catholic University of Valparaíso Institute for Architecture and that of the Hochschule für Gestaltung Ulm, which was founded five years earlier. It is a relevant comparison for several reasons, one of which is that a dominant figure at Ulm was a good friend and colleague of one of the key founding members of the Catholic University. Claudio Girola was born in 1923 in Rosario de Santa Fe, Argentina. Tomás Maldonado was born in 1922 in Buenos Aires. In 1945 they, together with Enio Iommi, Godofredo Iommi's brother, and others, founded the Asociación de Arte-Concreto and held their first exhibition in a gallery in Buenos Aires. Both men traveled through Europe where Girola worked with Georges Vantongerloo and Maldonado took a teaching position at the Technological University, Milan. In 1952, Girola returned to Argentina and Chile to participate in the founding and development of the Institute for Architecture in Valparaíso; Maldonado remained in Europe and accepted a teaching post at the Hochschule für Gestaltung Ulm in 1954, where he remained until its closing in 1968.

Both schools were founded as research institutes in a modern context. The Institute for Architecture in Valparaíso oriented its pedagogical research beyond the domain of the material and physical into the domain of the mind, using the modern poetic word and methodologies, and, therefore, was *set up* to engage modern culture through the mind. The Hochschule Ulm, on the other hand, oriented its research toward giving physical and material

A poetic act created July 1992 at the Open City with the poet
Godofredo Iommi, the sculptor Claudio Girola, and the students
and faculty of the Catholic University of Valparaíso. The poem's
first line reads "horizontals between earth and air."

form to all facets of modern industrial society, "to participate in the making of a new culture from spoon to city,"[9] as Max Bill formulated it, and to redefining the role of the designer in this society. Sociopolitical discussion was formulated through an engagement of modern technology, of mass production, which was to serve as the vehicle for redefining one's relationship to one's space. There was an overt preference for the use of the rational and, upon Max Bill's departure, science and scientific methodologies in the design process. The relationship between design, science, and modern mass production technologies produced the Ulm model, which was explored in collaboration with industry. As with the work of the Institute for Architecture, the research at Ulm required group collaboration and teamwork, but the group at Ulm comprised architects and designers in close association with scientists, research departments, marketing people, and technicians while the group in Valparaíso consists of architects, poets, painters, sculptors, and engineers. The Hochschule Ulm relied on industry to play a leading role in its process. The Institute for Architecture in Valparaíso rejects industry and professionalism because of the compromises they impose on the process, and it insists that the exploration of architectural space has nothing to do with the hypotheses and proofs of science because it is bound to discovery through the imagination. Architectural space must be reinvented each time—the *volver a no saber*—instead of proved viable through repetition of results.

The Hochschule Ulm's demise—resulting from a combination of many factors including a reliance on outside funding as well as internal strife between the designers, the theoreticians (the scientists), and the students caught in between—underscores important questions about this type of research, theoretical in nature, as it relates to science and to practice. A significant contributor to the longevity of the Institute for Architecture in Valparaíso is the fact that it consciously and consistently turns its back on architecture as a profession. Its graduates do operate as architects in the professional world, but the research and discussion of the school is conducted outside of that domain. Additionally, it does not attempt to reform the profession or society. Whereas the Hochschule Ulm maintained a rather positivist posture of reforming *society* through design based on functional determinism as it relates to *technology,* the research orientation of the Institute attempts to engage and reveal *culture* in a discourse with *space* through the creative mind ensnared by poetry.

9. *Max Bill as cited in Herbert Lindinger, editor, transl. David Britt,* Ulm Design, The Morality of Objects *(Cambridge: The MIT Press, 1991), 10.*

Walking wind pipes at the entry to the Open City and the Engi-
neer's House above

Although the research orientation and intentions of the Institute for Architecture are ambitious, there is a humility to both the approach and process because, believing in the validity of discovery, they allow things to appear. However, the research is also about preparation and provocation. Preparation requires a certain base of knowledge, a certain attitude, and even a certain morality. Detachment from that which is unnecessary and extraneous and an insistence on "doing" with what is sufficient prepare the ground for work, such as the Open City, to be approached from a pure posture in which the intention, the doing, and the material form operate as collaborators. In this morality, beauty is associated with the elemental, and wealth and power are rejected in favor of a "voluntary poverty."[10] The founders of the institute believe that too often grandeur is erroneously associated with wealth and power; grandeur, or that which is of greatness, comes from human effort and the exploitation of interior potentialities, which are only possible if one remains purely focused on the effort and the intention. Wealth and power pollute the effort and confuse the intention; therefore, poverty and economy are to be celebrated and cultivated.

This morality, as well as the emphatic detachment from the profession of architecture and pedagogic isolation from the other schools of architecture, lends a somewhat esoteric aspect to the institute and its members. It also has resulted in certain informal initiation rites, such as when several professors, on a trip by boat to the south, insisted that the students throw their identification cards, driver's licenses, and any other forms of artificially imposed personal identification into the sea.

3 *Arquitectura co-generada con la poesía, porque la palabra es inaugural, lleva, da a luz.*[11]

The central poetic preoccupation of the group, which was considered its "unconventional" approach, was the relationship of poetry to architecture, sculpture, and painting. It was to be a direct relationship, without mediating elements, and one which stated, and required, the bond of action to word. It was not poetry as a bias or sentiment but rather poetry as a way of acting and of doing creatively. The poetry around which the group united was that of the modern French poets—the *poètes maudits*—and of the surrealists: Baudelaire, Mallarmé, Rimbaud, Verlaine, Lautremont, Breton. This poetry involved a passionate quest in which poetry, no longer a commodity, transformed itself into poetic activity that aimed at recuperating the mind's

10.   Vittorio di Girolamo, "Lo Grande y Lo Bello De la Pobreza Voluntaria," El Mercurio (Santiago) 10 January 1993, E8-E9.

11.   "Architecture co-generated with poetry, because the word is inaugural, it conveys, it gives birth," Cruz, "Los Locos de Valparaíso," 49.

original powers. The poet was an alchemist who employed the imagination to transform reality both mentally and physically, who embraced the mystery and adventure of creative activity as reality was opened up to a different reading, a different understanding, a different reality, ignited by the power of words to embrace multiplicity and plurality within the unifying body of poetic language.

The appearance of the poètes maudits can be attributed to a confluence of two key conditions: first, the deterioration of the social status of poetry and poets as wealthy patrons of the nineteenth century disappeared in the wake of the growth of the European bourgeoisie, who were neither entertained nor enlightened by poetry. Poetry lost its value as a commodity, as a means of employment. Concurrently, there was the birth of modernity and a heritage of a vision of the modern world formed by the German romantics Hölderlin and Novalis in which divine systems were no longer sufficient or relevant to existential meaning within modern reality. Together, these provided the ground for the liberation of the poetic word from privileged claims and allowed it, in fact required it, to return to the source of language: to man. Man begins the return to himself for meaning and the responsibility that that implies. The "antagonism between the modern spirit and poetry begins as an agreement. With the same decision of philosophical thought, poetry tries to ground the poetic word on man himself. The poet does not see in his images the revelation of a secret power. . . . Poetic writing is the revelation of himself that man makes to himself." [12]

For this revelation to form, it was imperative that the traditional subject matter supplied by previous poetries be dismissed along with the emotionalism attached to such subject matter. The effusive description of elements of the natural world and the tedious articulation of feelings or thoughts supplied by these poetries were no longer relevant as they obscured the perception of reality. In the modern French poetry, reality and "real things" are not described but are consciously put aside so that transparent contact with the profundity of reality may be discovered. It is a self-conscious program that begins from an intuitive suspicion that our relationship with reality is attached not only to surface perceptions but, even more important, to an enigmatic mental dimension that underlies physical reality in which all things are linked by "correspondences" between them. Not through similarities but through Charles Baudelaire's idea of the almost mystical familiarity and intimacy between things that are never the same, that can never be the same. They are connected while retaining a distance that can

12. Octavio Paz, The Bow and the Lyre, trans. Ruth L. C. Simms (Austin, Texas: University of Texas Press, 1973), 215.

never be collapsed. Access to this unknown region is achieved by the imagination of the poet through its receptivity to the nonconcrete, through its use of language as a "forest of symbols" where mysterious and interconnected signs transport the mind and every sense.

Described as being "the original faculty of all human perception" by the English poet Coleridge, the imagination is capable of operating through reason, or of transcending reason, to perceive, select, judge, edit, transform. With the modern French poets, the making of poetic images combined with a necessary altering of language to discover as well as convey that which transcended reason. Words were not used to describe but to create images attached to the rhythm of language. For this reason, every new poem was to be a total recasting of its author's means of expression, disdaining all preestablished conventions and any innovations made prior to it in ways of thinking or ways of saying. Poetry was about discovery. It became adventurous. The fantastic and marvelous were stalked as the new poetry argued the reattachment of life to art: life consisting of the day to day, minute to minute, the mundane; and art being conceived through the word, specifically, because it is the element through which one engages both the world one acts within and the activity of the mind. It is a tool of perception and a tool of contemplation. Therefore, through the word, the poet is empowered to unite the processes of interpretation and transformation. "So we manage to have a synthetic attitude combining the need to transform the world radically and to interpret it as completely as possible."[13]

To achieve this interpretation and transformation, it was necessary to alter language radically. Its very matter was operated on as words were forced to "lay bare their hidden life and reveal the mysterious trade they indulge in, independent of their meaning."[14] It was asked to return to its origin, to discard the conventional relationship language had developed with meaning through arbitrary mental selection processes based on prescribed and learned value judgments. The "new" language was highly transparent and fluid, capable of joining sensation and thought by moving between the two with such facility as to totally obliterate the boundary between interior and exterior. It was to be, as Arthur Rimbaud described: "of the soul, for the soul, summarizing all, scents, sounds, colors, of thought hooking onto thought and pulling." The poem itself takes on an autonomous, ritualized quality as product of the imagination, and it becomes keyed to the participation of the reader as an experience in itself. Whereas poetry, the product, had previously been the ambition when it was marketable, it now becomes the by-product of poetic activity.

13. "Ainsi parvenons-nous à concevoir une attitude synthétique dans laquelle se trouvent conciliés le besoin de transformer radicalement le monde et celui de l'interpréter le plus complètement possible." André Breton, les vases communicants (Paris: Gallimard, 1955),

148. Translated into English by Mary Ann Caws and Geoffrey T. Harris under the title Communicating Vessels (Lincoln, Nebraska: University of Nebraska Press, 1990), 127.

14. André Breton, trans. Mark Polizzotti, Conversa-

tions: The Autobiography of Surrealism (New York: Paragon House, 1993), 83.

The Hospedería de la Entrada (the Entry Hospedería) the first building seen from the highway, is one of the first houselike buildings, called hospederías, built. As one moves around the building on the oblique, the collapsed space of the apparent gable end telescopes, revealing a five-bay wood structure whose enclosed spaces step up from the sand, releasing three staircases that descend from the house to touch the ground. Two move laterally outward, anchoring the house to the site, while the third spirals straight downward to attach to a cut in the ground through which a footpath moves on its way to the sea. A bowl is carved into the sand on the north side of the path forming a natural amphitheater. The path that connects the amphitheater to the highway and sea defines the course of the house while the roof planes are oriented toward the sun rising from the upper plateau. They simultaneously herald the rising sun and shelter the interior spaces from the forces of the southwesterly beach winds. The hospedería is about occupying the dunes, about the transparent qualities of the space and light over the sand, about the footpath that from the begin-

ning crossed the site, about the sun's movement off the plateau to the sea, about the maritime winds, and about the gesture of inhabitation with regard to house and the act of meeting in community.

It is important to understand the concept of hospedería, which is more than house. The word hospedería means inn and comes from the word huésped, meaning guest. The hospederia is a house that also serves the community by keeping its doors open to all guests. Although the family or inhabitants living in each hospedería regard the place as their home and are, in most cases,

the ones responsible for initiating the construction, its renovations, and additions, they do not own the structure or its site. These are owned by the community, and the inhabitants' role is seen as that of caretaker. This means that the hospederías are open to all those who may come, receiving food and/or lodging in exchange for a sharing of experiences and ideas. Each hospedería serves a civic purpose as well, which may include gatekeeper, banquet hall, or meeting ground.

The Entry Hospedería serves as a house with traditional spaces for sleeping, eating, socializing, and working, but it also serves the city by sheltering the hollowed-out communal amphitheater from the winds and by standing guard at the entrance to the Open City. At ground level adjacent to the hospedería a series of spaces serve as informal reception areas for entry and departure from the city. Here one finds a series of brick and concrete pivoting gate panels as well as a field of sculptural pipes that seem to be participating in some pagan ritual: a walking wind organ that converts the currents of air moving across the dunes into sound, transposing wind into tone that varies with direction and velocity.

Several other hospederías are found in the lowlands: two studio-workshop buildings, a retreat studio-house, music room, studio-exhibition building, tower, numerous agoras, sculptures, and built poems. Just beyond the entry gates is a crossing in the roadway. If one turns to the right, the northern spar of the sand road ends at two of the first hospederías to be built, which also host a third studio space within their rafters. Appearing today as a single building that is formally indistinguishable, the Banquet Hospedería was begun as two separate adjacent structures that grew in independent successive steps up/down and over/under one another, leaving a roundish void somewhere near the middle. Unlike the hospedería adjacent to the entry gates, the spatial articulation in the Banquet Hospedería that derives from the gestures of the inhabitants in relationship to space, surface, and site does not insert itself into an exterior built framework. Instead it derives from an internal and thematic logic that informs an intuitive process that is dependent upon the materiality and process of building. Building by simple addition of intuitive acts and not by the overlay or hierarchical

arrangement of design concepts has created a structure in which
there is a focus on spatial coincidences, on the translation of detached thoughts into distinct formal entities, and on the joints that
appear when two of these thoughts meet. The themes dealt with
in the hospedería are found as abridgments of issues faced
throughout the city: the sand, the sea, the memory of Valparaíso,
the sun, light, air, sound, the movement of the ground, passage,
the differentiation between and relationship of the elements that
form space with the elements that protect it from the elements,

and so on. Over the years, the Banquet Hospedería hospedería
has seen the most changes. Several years ago, because of problems of weather and water penetration, a roof was constructed
over the entire structure, transforming the hospedería's relationship to the sky and ground and making one acutely aware of the
prosaic drive of shelter, thus, elevating this prosaic drive to a level
of legibility—and with a certain naivety and nonchalance—so
that it engages the poetics inherent in its basic nature.

The hospederia named La Alcoba is formed by a series of interconnected alcove-like spaces spiraling around a central stair, which transports one from the ground to a deck aloft. The bulk of the house is supported above the sand by a series of vertical posts—masts—which are also used to stack billowed wall panels: a sand vessel that, however, does not carry one across the dunes but instead creates an experience in which the eye and its perception of phenomena crosses from one perception of the dunes to another. On the ground the dunes shelter from the winds and enclose one

among their undulations, introverted among their folds; from the deck aloft they become another sea, a surface of undulations perceived from above adjacent to the other sea, the Pacific. This "crossing" is strengthened by the fact that in the process of moving upward there are no windows facing outward to the sea. In fact the building completely turns its back to the sea. Light enters into the voids between the stacked curved wall panels either from above or reflected off of the sand from below, the curved surfaces serve to deflect and reflect the light. In La Alcoba, it is interesting that the communal element is the deck on top, meaning that passage through the hospedería is in contention with the privacy of house. Several years ago additional space was needed and constructed by extending the existing central stair tangentially, unfurling it on to the sand, and building space off of it. With this addition, the privacy of house was returned as a tangential occupation to the public possibility of passage to the upper terrace.

The Hospedería de los Diseños is initiated by the qualification and quantification of the phenomena associated with sand and light. The footpath through the dunes obliquely bisects a simple rectangular box of brick and wood. As the path enters the house it turns to brick. The blowing of the wind washes the sand into and out of the house, revealing more or less of the built path in a mimetic relationship to the waves and sand of the shore. The sand becomes another resident of the house, or a perpetual guest. Perpendicular

to and intersecting this path is a volume of light that rejoins the space that the path has ripped apart. Reattached to the body of the house by light, the major interior space is formed to create a perspectival focus down into the dunes, monitoring their movement, rather than open to the constancy of the sea. On the exterior of the hospedería, brick mediates between sand and wood and registers the migration of the sand, its rising and falling not dissimilar to the way in which the beach registers the tidal movement of the sea. The north face of the building, which faces the sea and light, is bleached white; the shadowed southern face, which gives to the upper dunes, is stained black.

Language engaged in poetic activity created poems in which the poet engaged in a mental communication with the world exterior to himself as well as an interior world. The poet becomes the medium between exterior and interior, and the poem becomes the site for the communication. The site that the poet creates contains both the object and the subject, the world and the poet, within its borders. By introducing the subject into the site of the poem, in a role more significant than that of narrator, modern poetry proclaims its commitment to reengaging us in a relationship with our world unmediated by divine systems or the false promise of reason's omnipotence. Subjectivity over reason's objectivity was part of the need to understand, or recreate, this relationship for the modern poet and, by extension, for modern society. Poetry was not personally motivated but aspired to reach into the *other* dimension of all human existence where we are positioned at the center of a "forest of symbols" that we initiated when we created language. Modern poetry embraced both the despotic ego and the id common to all men. It worked off of the assumption that the poet, as an individual in a certain cultural and historical context, is representative of the species of mankind in the same context and that the mental operation that consisted of going from being to essence on an individual level could discover value on a more general level. But, it is the poet who has the capacity to interpret and extend this value to restore to the species its integrity. "It is from poets, in spite of everything over the centuries, that it is possible to receive and permitted to expect the impulses that may succeed in restoring man to the heart of the universe, extracting him for a second from his debilitating adventure and reminding him that he is, for every pain and every joy exterior to himself, an indefinitely perfectible place of resolution and resonance." [15]

The absolute conviction in the power of poetry and poetic activity to interpret and transform life generated a consequent attitude toward poetry making, both as a craft and as a *sublime* activity. Mallarmé claimed that "Poetry is the expression, through human language restored to its essential rhythm, of the mysterious meaning of existence: it thus grants authenticity to our time on earth and constitutes the unique spiritual task." Included in the spiritual task were the poets and others who had the capacity to engage the poem with the imagination of the poet. No longer a commodity for wealthy patrons, religious or secular, and elevated out of the popular base it had lodged in during romanticism as well, poetry became an autonomous and even conflictive endeavor. It did not serve to entertain or enlighten but instead had the capacity to change life where other methods of revolution had

15. "C'est des poètes, malgré tout, dans la suite des siècles, qu'il est possible de recevoir et permis d'attendre les impulsions susceptibles de replacer l'homme au coeur de l'univers, de l'abstraire une seconde de son aventure dissolvante, de lui rappeler qu'il est pour toute douleur et toute joie extérieures à lui un lieu indéfiniment perfectible de résolution et d'echo." Breton, les vases communicants, 169–170; English translation: Caws and Harris, 146.

failed. It demanded that act be consequent with word. And, moreover, that poetry initiate action: "Poetry will no longer set its rhythm with the action, it *will be there in advance* [of the action]."[16]

For the modern French poets, the world's real torment lay in the human condition, much more so than in the social condition. Therefore, the action that was demanded was to be radical and extreme, but it was to be primarily transcendental in nature.[17] Poetry as revolution "shows a double face: it is the most revolutionary of revolutions and, simultaneously, the most conservative of revelations, because it consists only in reestablishing the original word."[18] From the German romantics Hölderlin and Novalis and onward, for all the European poets, the greatest promise of modernity was the spiritual liberation of humanity. Freed from the prescriptive powers of lords and kings, religion and its gods, the individual was now in possession of an authentic and unmediated relationship with his or her own life and death—this was the promise. The difficulty then becomes the responsibility of that freedom and a reordering of existential meaning in the modern era in which we have become distanced from ourselves and from others. Through the reestablishment of the original word and the reordering of language and its relationship to life, in a revolutionary manner, it was believed that the distance could be removed by revealing the alikeness and correspondences between things in a world no longer fractured or organized by systems of power.

Reestablishing the original word required a rediscovery of language, which meant that the process of making poetry, along with its reception, became more intuitive. A more subliminal use of language was initiated, and poetic form found a more consequent relationship with its subject matter. Rhetoric was relaxed if not completely abandoned as the poem engaged its potential as a vehicle for the spontaneous and discontinuous activity of the unconscious mind. Formally, one finds strong imagery elaborated by expressive sound patterns and nonrhyming rhythms that generate a feeling of spatial three-dimensionality. Free verse was initiated to strengthen the verbal transparencies and simultaneities as a complete shift from conscious activity to the discovery initiated by unconscious activity occurred.

Incited by the work of Freud, it became an assumption of the surrealist movement especially that the enigmatic dimension underlying reality was received through the unconscious mind. More than just receiving or reading this dimension, however, the motivation of the surrealist poets, as André Breton described it, was to find and fix the "point of the mind at which life

16. "la Poésie ne rythmera plus l'action; elle sera en avant." Arthur Rimbaud, "Lettre à Paul Demeny, 15 mai 1871 (Lettre du Voyant)," in Claude Edmonde Magny's Arthur Rimbaud Poètes d'Aujourd'-hui 12 (France: Pierre Seghers, Éditeur, 1956), 71.

17. Although the surrealists, because of their insistence on the reattachment of life to art and because of the revolutionary nature of their art, embraced the ideas of social revolution as delineated by Marxism, their dependency on pure subjective necessity over ideology placed them in a contentious contradictory position that eventually caused them to abandon the Communist group.

18. Paz, The Bow and the Lyre, 222.

and death, the real and the imagined, past and future, the communicable and the incommunicable, high and low, cease to be perceived as contradictions"[19] and to establish a conducting wire, *un fil conducteur,* between these two worlds too long disassociated. To achieve this, the constraints that weighed on supervised thought—the mind's subjection to immediate sensory perceptions that falsify the course of ideation, and the critical spirit imposed on language—had to be removed along with all obstacles created by mental logic, morality, and taste. Breton conceived of the subverting of the conscious mind and its closed rationalism, which is dominated by solicitations from the external world as well as by individual preoccupations and sentimentality, to release the imagination by making a direct link between poem and unconscious mind through psychic dictation. In the "First Surrealist Manifesto" he defines surrealism as psychic automatism: "psychic automatism in its pure state, by which one proposes to express—verbally, by means of the written word, or in any other manner—the actual functioning of thought. Dictated by thought, in the absence of any control exercised by reason, exempt from any aesthetic or moral concern."[20] Psychic dictation transcends the logic and reasoning processes of the conscious mind by exorcising intellectual activity and literary convention from the process. It employs language not merely as a means but allows it to exist as its own entity, relying on word play, verbal association, free tonal and audio association, original poetic analogies, chance associations, and so on. It exalts language as the material of the *fil conducteur.*

The surrealist program went beyond the poetic activity of the modern European poets in several aspects. First, poetry and the poem itself became even less important as the poetic experience broke the boundaries of all previous conventions related to this activity. For the surrealists, it was truly the experience and not the poem that took on value. Attached to this experience was the ambition to completely transform life in all its facets into poetry. Poetic activity engulfed all aspects and moments of life. It was an active transformation as well as an active revelation. Additionally, both the modern French movement and surrealism relied on subjectivity, but it was the surrealist group that inserted the subject so forcefully into the object that any vestige of objective reality was fractured beyond recognition. What is more, the imagination, which for the modern poets was a privileged tool belonging to the poet, became for the surrealists something that was "owned" and employed collectively. Therefore, ultimately, the subject disappeared as well. The concept of the poet as the prestigious interpreter and medium suffered

19.   André Breton, transl. Richard Seaver and Helen R. Lane, Manifestos of Surrealism (Ann Arbor: The University of Michigan Press, 1972), 123.

20.   Ibid., 26.

terribly at the hands of the surrealists, who believed that all men, being equal, have poetic capacity. Poetic capacity is the active foundation for inspiration and "the socialization of inspiration leads to the disappearance of poetic works, dissolved into life. Surrealism does not propose the creation of poems as much as the transformation of men into living poems."[21] The surrealist poets approached society and its historical context in a direct and open way, challenging both by their activity and their inactivity. There was no escape from life through the poem. Poetry was life and, more specifically, an attitude toward life in which inspiration was politic.

The surrealists, specifically the surrealist poets, used many different methods to spark the transmission along the "conducting wire" connecting the unknown regions of thought to the conscious mind. All of them relied on the self-conscious creation of an external context from which a spontaneous response or set of responses could erupt disassociated from conventional causality. Performances or "acts" were patterned after cabaret shows and entitled with sensational descriptions to entice a large audience participation. Dreamlike trance states were induced but were later abandoned when they became too dangerous physically. Excursions or wanderings were planned with gratuitous or nonexistent goals:

•

We all agreed at the time that great adventure was within our reach. "Leave everything. . . . Take to the highways": that was the theme of my exhortations in those days. . . . But what highways could we take? Physical highways? Not likely. Spiritual ones? Hard to imagine. Nonetheless, it occurred to us that we might combine these two types of roads. Out of this came a four-man stroll. . . . We started out from Blois, a town that we had picked at random on the map. It was agreed that we would head off haphazardly on foot, conversing all the while, and that our only planned detours would be for eating and sleeping. In actual practice, the project turned out to be quite peculiar, even fraught with danger. The trip, which was scheduled to last for about ten days, but which we finally cut short, immediately took an initiatory turn. The absence of any goal soon removed us from reality, gave rise beneath our feet to increasingly numerous and disturbing phantoms. . . . All things considered, the exploration was hardly disappointing, no matter how narrow its range, because it probed the boundaries between waking life and dream life.[22]

•

Games, too, whether written or spoken, were another very popular methodology because they required group interdependence, and they regenerated the receptivity of the group to immediate chance associations. Such games

21. *Paz,* The Bow and the Lyre, *226.*

22. *Breton,* Conversations, *59–60.*

were made up and played completely impromptu. Whether the joint creation of a deck of cards that would incorporate visual or word symbols for nonphysical entities such as love, dreams, revolution, knowledge, and so forth or the playing of *Cadavre Exquis* (the Exquisite Cadaver, or, the sketch of a cadaver), which refers to the child's game in which each participant contributes a piece of a body, in sequence, to a drawing without knowledge of the other parts, these games exemplified the purity of abstract thinking and creative activity. Freed from anticipated goals and desired results, they were after pure pleasure itself—the pleasure of communion through play. The discoveries they engendered came after.[23]

The influence of the surrealists and modern French poets on the founding and subsequent development of the pedagogical program and work of Alberto Cruz, Godofredo Iommi, and the faculty of the Institute for Architecture of the Catholic University of Valparaíso exists on a structural level and at several depths. Poetic acts, *travesías* (poetic voyages or crossings), and other methodologies engaged in by the members of the institute derive their structure from the methods of Breton and the poets of the modern French movement. Not unlike Breton's *psychic dictation* or the surrealist performance-like "acts," they are used, deliberately, to release the imagination from a programmatic and physical reality in order to relate architectural proposition to the poetics of space, context, and making through an intuitive process that taps into the same enigmatic mental layer related to the unconscious mind of which the modern French poets speak. From this, over time, an illusive thematic structure has appeared that becomes analogous to the enigmatic mental layer underlying reality, to Baudelaire's "forest of signs," or to the unpremeditated thematic obsessions of the surrealists. It is important to add that this illusive thematic structure is never formalized but remains open.

It is also important that this connection of architectural proposition to the underlying mental layer of reality, or to an illusive thematic base, is made through the word. The *poetic acts* are group meetings that occur on site and employ poetic methods to initiate the discovery and creative processes. To discover and generate "correspondences" between things—the physical site and space, the cultural site and space, space and form, form and materiality, space and gesture, gesture and construction, parts, components, and phenomena of each—in place of the singularity of concept making. They use words and the making of poetry, not merely an undefinable poetic bias, to stimulate the imagination. Words, because they have an immediate relationship with

23.   *André Breton, as cited by and commented on by Ingrid Schaffner, "Aprés Exquis," in the catalogue for "The Return of the Cadavre Exquis" (New York: The Drawing Center, 1993).*

our thought process and are capable of generating a multiplicity of images and dissimilar relationships concurrently. "The mind spins like an angel, and our words are the small shot that kills the bird."[24] Words have tremendous potential, through poetic means, to engage and promote spontaneous and random mental activity of a revelatory nature. Iommi qualifies this relationship: "Each human being has a gift which is speech. It is that which exists alive. Speech is transformed into language and continues to perfect itself until it arrives to the extreme maximum of tension, which is poetry. This poetic word is what serves as the foundation for architecture. Poetry, not as the inspiration, which is how it is used by most, but as the indicator [of direction]."[25]

The poetic acts take many forms from readings to games. In July 1992, I participated as spectator in one poetic act, a card game that took place in the Open City to determine the sites for a series of sculptures by Claudio Girola along the road leading to the Casa de los Nombres (see figs. 2.3–2.7). Twelve students from among the Catholic University faculty were selected to create, with Iommi, a poem that would indicate the sites among the dunes. To create the poem, images were drawn on twelve cards. They were then displayed one by one to be named by the students. One student would be selected at random to form a phrase or word from the image on the card. If the other students were in agreement, as a body, the phrase would be written on a blackboard; if anyone disagreed, the research with that card would start over. One card caused considerable difficulty until one student, out of frustration, said *"que se rompa"* (let it be torn up). The card was not torn up. "Que se rompa" became the next line to be written. Once the twelve lines were formed and written on the blackboard, Iommi began to work on the raw poem by adding punctuation to link words, break up phrases, break up words, cut lines into pieces, extend meanings. From the "finished" poem, Girola and the group were able to discover where to find the sites for the sculptures, which were then installed on the site.

The "discovery" is an interpretation of sorts and is part of an editing process that occurs naturally within the creative process. It is the moment when the poetic drive and the poetic opening is placed in a position of tension with the motivation and focus of the "project." It is one of the most interesting moments in the creative process because the tension is so significant while the moment in time is so slight. Editing and the electric tension produced between receptivity and activity was not a foreign issue to the surrealists. Breton's automatic writing depended on a strict decision to suppress

24.   "La Révolution Surréaliste," in George Melly and Michael Woods, Paris and the Surrealists (New York: Thames and Hudson, 1991), 76.

25.   "Todo ser humano tiene un don que es el habla. Es lo que existe vivo. El habla se transforma en lengua y se va afinando hasta que llega el extremo máximo de la tensión, que es la poesia. Esa palabra poética es la que sirve de fundamento para la architectura. La poesía no como inspiradora, que es como la usan todos, sino como indicadora." Godofredo Iommi, quoted by Margarita Serrano, "Godofredo Iommi," 12.

and annihilate the will and conscious activity to arrive at a completely passive and receptive state. It is debatable, however, that this state was ever accomplished; there was always an editing of sorts that took place even if it was merely the rejection of the results as unsuitable or trivial. Nevertheless, this does not invalidate what was and is accomplished. It does suggest that the nature and degree of the editing process is of paramount significance. It also suggests, since experience becomes a component of the process at this point, that there is a significant difference whether one or many are engaged in the editing. At the Open City, the editing process subscribes to the poetic intention. It attempts to remain pure by engaging experience through the collective engram.

Similar poetic acts are used for projects independent of scale or function. It is not an activity reserved for the special or obscure but for all activity, especially the mundane. And they transgress the borders of the immediate context through the concept of *travesía,* which is a poetic journey, of sorts, of discovery and revelation.

The propositioning of space, form, and tectonics through language and word, methodologically linked to the making of poetry as influenced by the surrealists, is part of a larger program of the institute in which the poetic word superimposes itself on traditional architectural and spatial discourse. More significantly, at the level of creative activity, it *replaces* this traditional discourse. Additionally, there is such a strong emphasis on creative activity as the basis for life that poetry virtually takes over as the motivating force of life. This was the intention in the founding of the institute, and it is consciously tied to the theoretical foundation of the modern French poets where men were to be "transformed into living poems."

But, beyond methodologies and theoretical intentions, the larger program is also influenced by the metaphysics of the modern French poetic movement. The critical questions that were posed by the German romantics and translated by the French poets become redirected in the work of the institute. The interrelationship of man, poetry, and history leads to visions— by Novalis, Blake, Mallarmé, Rimbaud, and others—of cultural and social reform, societies in which religion and utopian philosophies have been replaced by poetic action and actual communities dedicated to the collective production of poetry. As a community actively and radically dedicated to collective poetic activity, the influence of this vision on the institute is apparent. What is more significant is that the work of the institute redirects the question of "modern" man and his relationship to historical and cultural sites specifically onto Latin American man and his relationship to his historical and cultural sites. The condition the modern European poets faced was the world as a place in which new technologies and systems of knowledge, as well as a shift in the power base from church and state to industry, had distanced the poets from themselves, from others, from reality. The Latin American condition, which the work of the Catholic University of Valparaíso engages, is not as critically related to technology, knowledge systems, and industry but instead to the search for an authentic identity with regard to the world—a replacement for the identity given to Latin Americans by European self-interests. The question, the issue, the desire remains the same: meaning within the world and meaning grounded in man "revelation of himself that man makes to himself," but the site refocuses the imagination. It is in the work of the Catholic University of Valparaíso that the exploration of the question takes place, through written poetry as well as through architecture and sculpture—in space, form, and language.

4 *L'architecture est un acte d'amour et non une mise en scène. Que s'adonner à l'architecture, en ces temps-ci de translation d'une civilisation déchue dans une civilisation nouvelle, c'est comme entrer en religion, c'est croire, c'est se consacrer, c'est se donner.*[26]

One of the most striking aspects of the Institute for Architecture of the Catholic University of Valparaíso is not only the parallelism in the attitude of the faculty toward the living of life and toward the making of architecture—both attitudes employing poetry as the catalyst for activity—but also the depth and intensity of the commitment to activity. At the time of the reform of the school, Godofredo Iommi proclaimed that "the university must be erotic, if it is not erotic it stops to be a university."[27] He went on to explain to the somewhat surprised audience that Eros must be present in one's capacity to fall in love with the work that is done, in the passion that creation implies, and in the enjoyment that signifies the adventure of constructing life. In this attitude there is an absolute fusion of life and art that, in this case, is directed toward the making of space through architecture, and there is a devoted conviction to architecture as a creative endeavor occupying a rarified state of purity. This devotion is akin to religious devotion in its focus, strength, and passion and is born from an intention that is absolutely detached from architecture intended as a profession. The intention requires that artistic activity—creativity—discard formula and traditional canons and replace

26. "Architecture is an act of love and not a theatrical production. What can architecture give of itself in these times in which a decayed civilization is being transformed into a new civilization, it is as if to enter into religion, to believe, to devote oneself completely, to give oneself." Le Corbusier, entretien avec les étudiants des écoles d'architecture (Paris: les Editions de Minuit, 1957).

27. "La universidad tiene que ser erótica, si no es erótica deja de ser universidad." Godofredo Iommi, quoted by Margarita Serrano, "Godofredo Iommi," 9.

them with invention. To reinvent all, each time. And "to be grateful for a nonconventional way."[28]

This attitude and devotion to life as art is clearly affiliated with, and influenced by, the thoughts and words of the modern French poets. It is also influenced by the thinking of the modern French architect Le Corbusier, as outlined by several of his texts. In the first years of the founding of the institute, Alberto Cruz was engaged in copying the text of the *Oeuvre Complète,* word for word, and there is a distinct correlation between the words of Le Corbusier, specifically as found in the *Oeuvre Complète,* and the teachings and attitude of the founders of the architectural school in Valparaíso.[29] The modern French poets speak about life and art as it relates to poetry, and Le Corbusier moves, from a similar base, further into architecture. It is significant that the founders of the institute were influenced by the words of Le Corbusier, removing from the entire body of work its plastic qualities, which are clearly influenced by the "modern" promises of technology; extracting his attitude toward the making of architecture, toward creativity, and these in relationship to poetry and the poetic, from his forms and materiality. It is also significant that the textual material of interest to Cruz was the material that speaks about creative attitude, approach, intention, about a way of seeing, acting, doing, and not the more theoretical or prescriptive material.

Conspicuous correspondences between the founding attitudes and intentions of the Valparaíso school and the published words of Le Corbusier appear in the texts of two works in particular: the *Oeuvre Complète,* specifically volumes 1 through 6, and *Entretien Avec les Étudiants des Écoles d'Architecture.* Both volume 6 of the *Oeuvre Complète* and the *Entretien* were published in 1957, within five years of the founding of the institute. Le Corbusier considered the *Oeuvre Complète* his greatest work and one true legacy. Upon physical modification and removal of his built work and physical and critical modification or abandonment of unbuilt projects, it, alone, would remain indelibly as a description of his intentions within the creative process.[30] Its publication established a "spontaneous teaching of Corbu," although Le Corbusier himself, who abhorred academicism, would not teach.[31] The *Entretien* is unique in that it is one of the few instances in which Le Corbusier addressed students of architecture in a formal and somewhat pedagogic capacity, speaking about the passion, the creative process, and the proposition of architecture.

In the first volume, the first words of the *Oeuvre Complète,* Le Corbusier makes the founding statements of his attitude and intention. Architecture

28. "Agradecer de un modo no convencional," Alberto Cruz's first words in front of the School of Architecture of Chile for the conferring of the Prize of Honor in 1975; Browne, "Amereida," 79.

29. Conversations with Guillaume Jullian de la Fuente, who was a student in the first class to graduate from the Institute of the Catholic University of Valparaíso and, later, chef d'atelier for Le Corbusier, 1957–1965.

30. Ibid.

31. "En 1927, un 'enseignement Corbu' spontané s'est établi avec la publication de 'L'OEuvre Complète L. C.' à Zurich, par Willy Boesiger." Le Corbusier, entretien avec les étudiants.

is not a profession, it is not a "career," and it is connected to the poetic. "I want architects to become the very elite of society—men with the richest intellects and an intelligence open to everything. Architecture is a habit of mind, not a profession."[32] Architecture demands a clear formulation of the problems to be faced. Everything depends on that, for this formulation is the decisive factor. Are we to limit those problems simply and solely to the satisfaction of utility? If so we must first start by defining utility. Do poetry, beauty, and harmony enter into the life of modern men and women; or must we consider its scope as being confined to the mechanical performances." The implication through these questions is that poetry, for Le Corbusier, belongs to the status of utility. It is explicitly of use to modern men and women. The use of the word utility (*utilité*), with its mundane connotations, further implies that poetry is perhaps even a necessity of modern life. It is not something rarefied, extraneous, or marginal. Poetry inserted into life—not a luxurious commodity.

In the introduction to volume 6 of the *Oeuvre Complète,* Le Corbusier further qualifies the relationship of the poetic, specifically, to the formulation of architecture. He speaks of "a common denominator: the 'plastic incident' and moreover: 'the poetic incident.'" And, he relates architecture and the poetic to art and to the unknown.

•

This being the case it only remains to decide whether occupying one's self with poetic phenomena, manifested by volume, color, and rhythm, is an act of unity or one of chaos—whether architecture, sculpture, painting, that is to say volume, form, and color are incommensurable or synchronous—synchronous and symphonic. And whether life . . . can but touch unknown existences along its path, by the means that one commonly calls "art." The dictionary says that art is "the manner of doing." . . .

Ladies and Gentlemen, the heart of the matter is this, . . . that one strives (from time to time—exceptional days!) to qualify the indefinable, a word which describes one of the paths to happiness, and which, extraordinarily, is not translatable into certain languages. [In those things which are not of the countenance but of the essence, the architectural destiny is played out.] [33]

•

Clearly, the notion of the poetic as related to the "indefinable"—a word which is, itself, illusive—and to that which is of the "essence" as opposed to the "countenance," is part of the intellectual and cultural atmosphere created by the modern French poets and the surrealists. Part of what made Le Corbusier unique among the architects of the modern era was that he, unlike many

32. *Godofredo Iommi echoes this when he says: Pero nosotros no queríamos hacer la carrera. Teníamos un movimiento de resistencia a todo eso. (For us we did not want to make a career. We had a movement of resistance against all this.) In Serrano, "Godofredo Iommi," 10.*

33. *"En ces choses qui ne sont pas d'aspect, mais d'essence, se joue précisément le destin architecturale." I have inserted this from the entretien avec les étudiants des écoles d'architecture as a parallel thought.*

of his colleagues, was breathing in this air, and it became a significant part of his personal vision, not only for inspiration but as a way of acting. Additionally, some of his writings, notably *Le Poème de l'angle droit* (1955), are very much poetic works in the modern vein. *Le Poème de l'angle droit* is extremely significant in that it fuses poetry, the plasticity of painting, the poetics of architecture (modern architecture) relative to the natural world, and personal mythologies within its vision of the world.[34] For Le Corbusier there is a certain equivalence between the poetic and the plastic, and therefore the relationship between poetry and plastic form is, theoretically, an unmediated one, or one mediated by the individual architect; it is a personal vision. Whereas for the founding members of the Catholic University of Valparaíso, the relationship between the poetic and the plastic is mediated by the word, by language. The word dominates the activity, which is not personal but pedagogic activity. It is group research partially influenced by the personal vision of Le Corbusier as it focused on creativity.

Returning to the text cited above:

•

Evidently the problem is to cut through the complexities, to attain simplicity. To cut through the chaos of life, to pursue an inspiring dream: not one that remains young, but one that becomes young.

•

The dream that "becomes young" is closely linked with a creative process that maintains a commitment to the posture of invention while building on its own continuity and the memory of itself—reinvention. In the *Entretien* Le Corbusier explains that each time the *feuillet blanc* (the blank page) demands a reinvention of the architectural proposition or the act is not a creative one. Without much doubt, the erased footsteps in the sand of the institute's concept of *volver a no saber* are analogous to the *feuillet blanc* of which Le Corbusier speaks. Both implicate reinvention in the design process, which, itself, relies on the imagination or the image-making and collating process. Furthermore, the imagination is creativity fused with memory. Memory, not knowledge. Knowledge fuels prescriptions and formulas, while memory fuels the imagination. It is for this reason that Le Corbusier passionately supports experience over academicism.

In both the first volume of the *Oeuvre Complète* and in the *Entretien,* Le Corbusier associates invention with "the courage and particular creative energy attached to things in which reason and poetry coexist, where an alliance between wisdom and enterprise is made."[35] He sees academicism as

34.   Richard A. Moore, "Alchemical and Mythical Themes in the Poem of the Right Angle, 1947–1965," Oppositions 19/20 (Winter/Spring 1980).

35.   "le courage et le génie créatif tout particulièrement attaché aux choses ou coexistent la raison et la poésie, ou font alliance la sagesse et l'enterprise." Le Corbusier, entretien avec les étudiants.

exclusive of invention. "Let us not deceive ourselves: academism is a way to not think which suits those who fear the hours of anguish of the invention, no matter that they are compensated for by the hours of joy of the discovery."[36] Academicism, in its search for truth and knowledge, treats history as a dead and untranslatable entity instead of as a living entity that can give of itself—through the process of remembering, not historicizing—to the creative process. And, it is academicism that disregards completely the teachings of the natural environment. In a letter addressed to a group of modern architects in Johannesburg in 1936, published in the *Oeuvre Complète* 1910–1929, Le Corbusier talks passionately against academicism, about history, and the creative process.

•

Though I have to admit that my own hands are soiled by the scourings of past centuries, I prefer washing them to having them cut off. Besides the centuries have not soiled our hands. Far from it they have filled them. . . .

Study of the past can be fruitful provided we abandon academic teaching and let our curiosity wander across time and space to those civilizations, grandiose as modest, which have expressed human sensibility in a pure form. Architecture must be torn away from the drawing board to fill our hearts and heads. . . .

How are we to enrich our creative powers? Not by subscribing to architectural reviews, but by undertaking voyages of discovery into the inexhaustible realm of Nature! . . . Open your eyes, burst the strait-jacket of professional discussions! Devote yourself so wholeheartedly to studying the meaning of things that architecture spontaneously becomes an inevitable consequence.

•

Abandonment of academic teaching and academicism, removing oneself from the theoretical seduction of the drawing board, discovery through travel, and the rejection of professional discourse are important elements of the Catholic University of Valparaíso. They refer to a general attitude that embraces experience as an active endeavor and theoretically rejects knowledge as the unique basis for a way of acting and doing. Since experience is subjective, this attitude assures the supply of material to the imagination, which connects physical reality to an individual's own translation of phenomena. The theory then follows that when the individual becomes part of a group, the subjective material coming from multiple, but not dissimilar, experience is distilled to its most essential state. It does not become objective. Rather, it is subjective ether.

36. "Ne nous illusionnons pas: l'académisme est une manière de ne pas penser qui convient à ceux qui craignent les heures d'angoisse de l'invention, pourtant compensées par les heures de joie de la découverte." Ibid.

Parenthetically and risking oversimplification, it is possible to discuss the influence of the modern French poets, surrealists, and Le Corbusier on the theoretical underpinnings of the institute by using the metaphor of the juxtaposition and interdependence of night and day found so often in poetry and in the work of Le Corbusier. The influence of the surrealists, in a certain sense, provides the nocturnal methodology: passive receptivity of unconscious thought and, through this thought, connection to the *other* side of thought and existence. On the other hand, the influence of Le Corbusier's writings incites the diurnal: active solicitation of experience. The two are bound together in the changing light of an atmosphere in which poetics has replaced oxygen.

Additionally, beyond the creative approach, there is the enormous topic of nature and its role in the writings and plastic work of Le Corbusier as it has influenced the theoretical and physical work of the Institute for Architecture of Valparaíso. The founders of the school understood completely, as did Le Corbusier, that a society becomes disabled if it loses and breaks "the contact between its material way and the natural elements which belong to its spiritual direction. Rupture of the contact between goals and ways, absence of a line of conduct."[37] And there clearly are more direct influences on the work of the institute as well, or at least noteworthy correspondences: the notion of the 24-hour daily cycle as a delineator of both space and time, creating the site for human occupation of space, and thereby establishing the beginning point of urban activity. But these influences have been merged with other influences coming from the Latin American culture and physical landscape: from its relationship to Spanish and Amerindian cultures, from the specific physical environment of South America, from the space of Chile, from the city of Valparaíso.

El camino no es el camino.[38]

Given that the physiography of Chile is so powerful and diverse, with high deserts, green valleys, and broken land wedged between fjords and glaciers— a seam between mountain and sea—and, especially, because the founding position of the institute set forth a pact of loyalty to this Latin American context and the Latin American condition, one must ask, at some point, why the modern European intellectual movement had such significance for the founders and members of the institute. Clearly Europe was a center of gravity for artistic and intellectual activity at the beginning and middle of the twentieth

37. "le contact entre son train matériel et les éléments naturels de sa conduit spirituelle. Rupture de le contact entre buts et moyens, absence de ligne de conduite." Ibid.

lommi, amereida (Valparaiso: School of Architecture of the Catholic University of Valparaíso, 1967), 189.

38. "The road (way) is not the road (way)." Godofredo

century. But it was France and especially Paris that attracted the Latin American artists, writers, poets, and architects. Vincente Huidobro, Pablo Neruda, Matta—each had his own romance with Paris.

The Latin American continent's relationship with Europe is a complex one that belongs to the history of the Americas. It is a history of emulation and denial, colonialization and independence. The repudiation of Spain that led to the American wars for independence (1808–1810) instigated a general condition in which a passionate search for identity, among the intellectuals, reverberated throughout the South and Central American continent. But a certain dependence on Europe as the source of their colonial heritage meant that any search for identity could not deny Europe entirely. Latin America is just that: a joining of the Latin culture with the pre-Hispanic American cultures and the physical site of the Americas. The repudiation of Spain, therefore, was not a repudiation of Europe and all things European. In fact, it required a surrogate, which it found in France. Latin America turned toward France as "the new source of liberty, taste, Romanticism, and all things good. Typically, a Chilean historian, Benjamin Vicuña Mackenna, wrote from the French capital in 1853, 'I was in Paris . . . the capital of the world, the heart of humanity . . . the universe in miniature.' And the Brazilian aristocrat Eduardo Pardo was quoted as saying with a sigh, 'Without a doubt, the world *is* Paris.' In the sixteenth century Spanish America had been the Utopia of Europe. Now we returned the compliment and made Europe the Utopia of Spanish America. Guatemala City even called itself 'the Paris of Central America.' Our secret yearning, of course, was that one day Paris would call itself 'the Guatemala City of Europe.'"[39]

France was the general focus of Latin American European longing, but Paris was the place of activity, modern activity, and the seat of the modern poetic movement that was engaged in an active metaphysical search of its own, driven by questions and needs similar to the Latin American quest for identity. Spain and Spanish poetry offered little of relevance to the modern Latin American writers, poets, and artists not only because of their need for political, intellectual, and psychological independence but also because the poetry of Spain did not participate in the modern poetic movement. It could not take part because the idea with which the movement was impregnated, that poetry was to be a "revelation of himself that man makes to himself," was completely foreign to the Spanish tradition. Modern poetry was, specifically, to be a revelation independent of religion, and the Spanish poetic tradition was absolutely steeped in Spanish Catholicism, which it would not

39.   *Carlos Fuentes,* The Buried Mirror: Reflections on Spain and the New World *(New York: Houghton Mifflin, 1992), 278.*

relinquish. "Solemnity and pathos had numbed the muscles of Spanish poetry," while French poetry surged forward into unknown territories. It was
modern Latin American poetry, in fact, that revived the Spanish language
poetically through its embrace with the French poetic movement.[40]

Modernism, as a vision, was vivacity and cosmopolitanism. The promise of a future present in the now. This meant the presence of an intensity of
activity, creative as well as industrial. From the perspective of Latin America,
Paris provided a vision of a new world open to the future. Paris was modernism incarnate, vital and passionately alive with creative force. For the
founders of the Catholic University of Valparaíso the words and intentions of
the French poets (and of Le Corbusier) "did not have roots."[41] They were
new, without precedent, and full of possibilities. Their influence provided
the theoretical and metaphysical base from which the work and pedagogical
program of the institute formed, while the space and physical phenomena of
Chile and the South American continent provided the physical foundation.
The work of the school has become the site of confluence between the two.

⑤ *En arquitectura cualquier necesidad humana se desarrolla en el espacio.*[42]

The action and morality that was demanded by the founding attitudes of the
faculty of architecture—the reconnecting of goals and ways, of word and
act—led to a very different way of working and teaching at the Catholic University of Valparaíso. It was a way of working that removed the students from
the drawing boards and lecture halls and bound them to the city as laboratory. Alberto Cruz emphasized that "the architects are those that in life know
how to read, know how to build the countenance which the space holds."[43]
To understand architecture as the container or skin for the "countenance"
of space required divesting space of a superficial relationship to function in
order to discover its more intimate relationship with the phenomena it
engages. For this discovery it was necessary to go into the city, to travel
through it, to read it; to see how the space engages and holds these acts of
life; how it accommodates, accumulates, and articulates the gestures. It required entering all the spaces, grand and small, all the nooks and crannies,
and it required the observation of phenomena as they relate to space. Observation was made through drawing. Rapid sketches that bypass intellectual
analysis and taste to allow the eye to see through the gesture of recording
were, and are, fundamental. They are a tool of intuitive analysis and a way of
discovering the subject as well as the object. Unlike photographs, they record

40. *Octavio Paz in* The Siren and the Seashell, *translated by Lysander Kemp and Margaret Sayers Peden (Austin, Texas: The University of Texas Press, 1976) writes specifically about the relationship of the Latin American poets to their origins and to the modern movement in France. How the poetry of the Latin American poets, spe- cifically that of Rubén Dario, "made Spanish verse the point of confluence between the an- cestral background of American man and European poetry. At the same time it uncovered a buried world and re-created*

the ties between the Spanish tradition and the modern spirit" (p. 30).

41. *From a discussion among the travelers as recorded in the travel log of the institute's first* travesía *in* amereida volumen segundo *(Valparaíso: School of Architecture of the Catholic Uni- versity of Valparaíso, 1986), 168.*

42. *"In architecture all hu- man necessity unfolds in the space." Alberto Cruz, as quoted in the second-year studio note- book of Guillaume Jullian de la Fuente, 1952.*

Valparaíso

within themselves the mind and eye of the individual sketching. They record the act of seeing, not just what is seen. They serve the act of seeing by demanding a precision to the observation and by transferring the observation to memory. In so doing, a foundation is established within memory that can be accessed for the creative process. This type of drawing serves analysis that is not truly analytical. Rather, it is a transfer of information from physical construction to mental construction—to mental image in which the critical phenomenological and spatial information has been filtered out from the "picture" through the eye and its unmediated relationship to the mind, not through taste and convention. It is a way of recording that is not dissimilar to the observational sketches of Le Corbusier.

The city in which the students of the institute work to research the "countenance of the space," and which influences much of the subsequent design work including the work at the Open City, is the city of Valparaíso. Valparaíso is a city with a very strong spatial presence as the result of how one occupies, how one finds space on, a site whose topography is emphatic and a challenge to the right-angle posture of human occupation of space. It is a city of extraordinary beauty, and structural and gestural complexity.

The built city erupts from a half-moon-shaped, north-facing basin on the Pacific Coast thirty-three degrees below the equator. It occupies a small portion of flatland as a system of gridded streets running parallel and perpendicular to the coast. These streets are defined mostly by nineteenth-century stone buildings that demonstrate their ambitions to be European. Newer buildings of masonry or steel have been built into holes in the fabric produced by the selective demolition of various earthquakes. Formal, often highly decorated and overscaled, the older buildings stand with the newer buildings in strong contrast to the nonchalant maze of construction that covers the hills. These hills overlay the flatland like long fingers spread out on the land, pushing and shoving the grid system to conform. One band of hills numbers over a dozen and defines the southern and southwestern edges of the flatland. Another band defines the eastern edge and is severed from the first group by a major road that links Valparaíso and the northern coastal towns, including Ritoque, to the capital city, Santiago.

The city of Valparaíso is like two cities whose formal and poetic structures are defined by a series of relationships and architectural elements determined by the specifics of topography and settlement. The "downtown" is determined by an imported formal program and classical principles of grid, axis, plaza, court, periphery, linear movement, object in field, et cetera, with

43. "Los architectos son aquellos que de la vida saben leer, saben construir el rostro que tiene en el espacio." Alberto Cruz, quoted by Enrique Browne, "Amereida: una experiencia arquitectónico—poética chilena," 75.

color and informality provided by the human traffic. In contrast, the "up-town" responds to prosaic needs for making space on sixty-degree slopes that are often destabilized by earthquakes while, inadvertently, engaging the poetics of sea, sun, and horizon. The uptown is apparent disorder with the topography determining location, orientation, geometry, and structure of building. The buildings twist and turn to conform to the slope, and the roads exist as serpentine paths running along the crests of the hills or leaping into the voids between the hills to attach to the city below. The oblique, diagonal, and nonrectilinear rule. Roofs become terraces and new ground. The sky and sea become space. Everywhere there are reminders of the inhabitants' tenuous hold on the horizontal. Reminding one of the dependence on the sea for livelihood are the countless balconies looking out to the Pacific. And then there are the earthquakes, which direct the construction methods and materiality of the buildings: light, wood framed, with corrugated metal siding and roofing to move with the motion of the ground and resettle mostly unharmed into their static state.

Linking the architecture of the two cities are regional generalities of climate, light, culture, and history that inform every building. Physically and spatially, the uptown and downtown are tied together by funiculars, miradors (overlooks), slots of space formed between buildings that focus to the sea from above and to the hills from below, inclined planes out of which the streets and sidewalks emerge, color, and the ubiquitous staircase. The Chilean poet Pablo Neruda writes of Valparaíso:

•

But others never made it to the hilltops, or down below, to the jobs. They put away their own infinite world, their fragment of the sea, each in his own box. . . .

Stairways! No other city has spilled them, shed them like pearls into its own history, down its own face, fanned them into the air and put them together again as Valparaíso has. No city has had on its face these furrows where lives come and go, as if they were always going up to heaven or down to the earth. . . . If we walked up and down all of Valparaíso's stairways, we will have made a trip around the world.[44]

•

Valparaíso is a city of fragments whose unity exists as a mental reconstruction of the parts. It is a city of fragments in the way the building fabric is completely disrupted by the irregularities—the twists and turns—of the topography. And a city of fragments in the spatial experience as well: one does not find grand vistas or traditional plazas that orient the eye but finds instead slots of space that turn into the fabric, reorienting themselves many times

44. *Pablo Neruda, trans. Hardie St. Martin,* Memoirs *(New York: Viking Penguin, 1987). See pp. 55–64 for his description of Valparaíso.*

over as one travels up and down the staircases, up and down the roads or parallel to the slope. Views are tall framed clips of pieces of the city set up again by the twists and turns of the topography. The city is fragmented also in the way in which it is occupied. No longer the prosperous and wealthy city of trade it was prior to the opening of the Panama Canal, and no longer fully occupied, the result is the partial inhabitation of larger houses or their being split among multiple residents—each of whom modifies, in an ad hoc manner, their part with color, access, additional constructions and subtractions. Like a detective novel, the city is only known and discovered through reconnecting the pieces as one encounters them.

When the new school began, in the first semester of the first-year class, Cruz gave an assignment to locate a specific building in Valparaíso from a photograph. Each student was given a different photograph. During the semester, the students recorded their search and their encounters with the city. At the end of the semester some students returned to continue in architecture while others, because of their experiences, became poets, musicians, sculptors, mathematicians. Research in the city directed from a phenomenological and poetic bias had facilitated not only discovery of the city's spatial countenance but also a place of beginning for each student. This is very important given the insistence on creativity and invention in the design process. Each student's context is his or her own creative continuity rather than the accident of class enrollment and composition. Students are judged upon their personal development from semester to semester in the context of their own work as an entirety; final juries for each semester require the presentation of the previous semesters' work for review. Simply presenting a good project is not sufficient for success, and students have been held back for drawing too well while thinking too little.

For this reason—the emphasis on individual creativity and continuity—the school was organized around ten semesters that are determined more by "tasks" than by "sections"; the tasks include students of different years. Because there are no formal studio spaces within the institute, the students work outside of the school, further amplifying their dependence on the city as laboratory while simultaneously provoking creative and critical independence. Weekly meetings are held in which the entire school comes together to discuss the tasks with regard to the work generated and the goals of the projects. The methods for teaching do not preclude architectural assignments that are traditional in nature (housing, community buildings, urban design, et cetera); however, they focus on the integration and synthesis of observation and consequent design activity through conceptual work and ideation built in drawing and in writing. The ideation is part of a mental process that is undertaken with rigor and precision in mind while simultaneously recognizing the value of the intuitive to design as discovery. It requires the cooperation of the intuitive and the critical capacities of the mind.

Throughout the process, it is clear that there is a reliance on intuition as one research tool. The written word with its poetic and critical capacities is another tool. Early projects of the school demonstrate the fruitful dialogue developed between words/text and architectural/spatial/formal research. Often the text is structured poetically and is responsible for setting up the questions of the research and for delineating or limiting the task. "Why name them, why put names [words] to them [the tasks]? Because the words announce a specific goal. They are there at the beginning and at the end of the work: it is the words which judge what has been realized."[45] In essence, the words create the mental site of the project. In these projects the text cannot be separated from the drawn architectural proposal; they are completely interdependent. The projects use the text as a poetics and for the delineation of a sequence of questions about architectural space and form as they relate to phenomena, experience, and even the place of technology in culture. One reads the project in the space between the text and drawings. It is there that the architectural proposition lies. The drawn project does not answer the questions but serves as their formal and spatial elaboration. Nor does the text attempt to explain or describe, or justify, the project but merely attempts to set up the critical dialogue of the proposition, which is an architectural proposition, not a critical proposition.

It seems that one can see within the structure of the pedagogical approach of the architecture studios a certain classical or traditional model that has, however, been infected and pedagogically transformed by its bias toward the poetic. The emphasis on work that arises as a consequence of research, specifically, research based on observation of how space phenomenologically engages human activity, is a symptom of the influence of the poetic bias. At the same time, in the creation of text poetically formed and motivated, and integrated into the architectural process, is the actual presence of the poetic imagination. However, where the interrelationship and interdependency of poetry and architecture becomes even more significant is in the research conducted parallel to the formal studios where poetic space overlaps into architectural space through the introduction of the "poetic act" or *phalène*.

45. "¿Por qué llamarlas, por qué poner nombres? Porque las palabras nos señalan una tarea. Ellas están al comienzo y al fin de la obra: son ellas las que juzgan lo realizado." Alberto Cruz in the text for his project for the Chapel los Pajaritos in 1952–53.

Fundamentos de la Escuela de Arquitectura (Santiago: Universidad Católica de Valparaíso, 1971).

Although not specifically a pedagogic tool, and never having been formally structured into the teaching of the school, the *phalène* nevertheless provides a forum for liberation of thinking. In the later works of the school—including and, especially, the Open City—the *phalène* has taken on such significance in its capacity to consummate the relationship between poetry, architecture, and life that it validates the pedagogic assumption that poetry can provide the base for a privileged way to knowledge.[46]

Phalène is a French word for a species of butterfly. It was used by Edgar Allan Poe to equate poetry with the flight of the butterfly attracted by starlight. Not unlike a nocturnal Icarus, the butterfly knows that reaching the star will mean its own death but, despite this, it is unable to alter its course. The *phalène* developed out of a series of seminars given by Iommi on modern poetry and art. Because modern poetry was not intended as an elitist preoccupation, and it was to be of and for life, the students were incited to take the poetry out of the classroom and into the city. They recited poems in the streets, on the buses, in the hills, on the beach. No longer spectators, they entered into the life of the city as participants, and they engaged poetry as participants. These recitations, almost always done in a group, developed into the *phalène* or poetic act. Many of the original *phalènes* were extremely provocative and radical interventions into the unsuspecting urban life of Valparaíso because the poetic base that was established insisted upon the "changing of life" and not merely "changing life." Not to change one's course in life or exchange one life for another but to change that which is at the very heart of life: its essence, its purpose, and the way of living it.

Originally an opportunity to recite poetry, the phalène, in very little time, evolved into something more ambitious; it became a way to make poetry as well and, therefore, to engage language in the act of creation. These poetic acts take on several forms: recitations, improvised performances, group writings of poetry, card games, tournaments. They are always done in a group, and they provoke the interaction of architects, engineers, sculptors, painters, poets, and others around language absorbed in poetic activity. Like the surrealist acts, they provide a medium for intuitive and subliminal interpretation and transformation. For the members of the Valparaíso school, this interpretation is integrally linked to the place in which the act unfolds. This, combined with the fact that the *phalène* is an active participation in poetry made by a group that occupies space of a certain quantity, in a certain configuration, and articulated by the occupation and movement of the human

46. Fernando Pérez-Oyarzún, "The Valparaíso School," The Harvard Architectural Review, vol. 9 (1993), 88.

Phalène on the beach in Horcón near Valparaíso in which the epic poem La Araucana *by Alonso de Ercilla was recited. (From the Catholic University of Valparaíso-UCV-archives.)*

Water Tower at the Open City, 1988

activity participating in the poetry, introduces the possibility of *linking poetry to place and to space:* to the place in which it occurs and to the space which it configures. It is precisely in service of this that the poetic act achieves its status as initiator of the architectural process.

6 *Comienza una nueva era de la historia con la epifanía de américa—un lugar misterioso donde se dieron todas las razas del mundo rendez-vous por la primera vez desde la división de la torre de babel.*[47]

Prior to 1965 the action that was demanded by the founding attitudes of the Catholic University of Valparaíso translated into poetic activity that focused its research on the city and surroundings of Valparaíso. By the late 1960s the group of people working together grew from nine to over thirty members and consequently became a driving force of significant proportion. Its momentum began to grow. In 1965, the *amereida* was written by Godofredo Iommi as an articulation of intentions and approach. As a poem that poses a critical set of questions about the Latin American heritage, it introduces to the work of the Catholic University's faculty of architecture a re-presentation of the historical and cultural context of the New World. In essence, through the questions it poses and debates for itself, it translates a closed history, as written, into history as poetic memory open to rediscovery. It is that memory that the architects, artists, and poets of the Catholic University employ in order to create. The poem has proved itself to be a manifesto of great importance to the work of the school, and it serves as an informal charter as well for the Open City in Ritoque, also named Amereida.

Formally, the *amereida* follows in the footsteps of the modern French poets with its free verse, lack of punctuation, and visual as well as tonal composition. In the *amereida,* as in Apollinaire's *Calligrammes,* the visual form on the page coalesces with the poetic content, augmenting the meaning derived from the rhythms. Blank spaces surround and intrude in the verse, forming a relationship with the syntactic units and leaving space for the mind of the reader to participate. Punctuation is erased so as not to interfere with the wanderings of the imagination and the migration of phrases through and into each other.

The central theme of the poem is discovery of fatherland in the new world. It is about recovery of the trail, of the connection back, both to the earth in the form of the South American continent, its rivers, mountains

47. *"A new era of history [or, the story] begins with the epiphany of america—a mysterious place where it is said that all the races of the world meet for the first time since the division of the tower of babel,"* Godofredo Iommi, *amereida,* 165.

and forests, and to the origin of the Latin American people as a mixture of races and voices. It questions the beginnings, motives, and creation of Latin America. The *amereida* is a poem of longing and, more important, a poem of action as well in that it proposes the discovery of the Latin American status specifically through poetic action.

The first part of the poem reframes the question of the "discovery." It begins with the question "no fue el hallazgo ajeno a los descubrimientos?" (was not the finding alien to the discoveries?)[48] The word "alien" in the middle sets up the distance between "finding" and "discoveries," and its semantic properties further distance the two terms—that both terms are foreign to each other and therefore irreconcilable; that finding is not the same as discovering and vice versa—creating a space of tension between the notion of finding and of discovering, between what was expected and what was found. Contained within the space generated by that primary question is an implication of the contradiction that lies at the heart of the Latin American condition: the difference between motives and events, or, in this question, *an event* that forced a revision not only of motives and purpose but even of the metaphysical perception of the world as constructed by the European clergy and scientists.[49] Within the space of the difference between finding and discovering is also the implication of a bifurcation of possible destinies: one destiny attached to the object as it was expected to be and another that misbehaves, which constantly surprises and mystifies. The destiny of the Latin American continent, taking the latter route, unfolded and unfolds still, despite the motives and intentions of the "discoverers." The "destiny awakened gently from this gratuity of error and is opening still."[50] Yet, it is still attached to the events of the discovery and its aftermath, to the turmoil that was generated as the European world vision was challenged and transformed by the appearance of the "new world," to the conquest.

From the first question the poem builds more questions about the heritage of the Americas, about destiny and identity. It implicates both the Latin Europeans, with their ghosts, and those who inhabited the continent before, with their idols, in the destiny of the continent as well as the physical presence of the land itself. And it claims that, because of their nostalgic propensity, the inhabitants of Latin America are caught between the imitation of idols and of ghosts. Either way it is not an authentic existence but one of imitation: "the people of america, between idols and ghosts, we are only imitating."[51] The poem proposes the search for an authentic existence

48.   *Hallazgo refers to the object found and the act of finding. Ibid., 3.*

49.   *Edmundo O'Gorman, The Invention of America (Bloomington, Indiana: Indiana University Press, 1961) discusses how the encounter with the unsuspected mass of land* that would become the New World forced a complete revision of not only the long-held physical understanding of the world but also the metaphysical vision of the world as it was upheld by the religious powers. Because of its location and magnitude, the mass of land encountered did not fit neatly into the existing concept of the world in which only Europe, Asia, and Africa were considered to be the insular components of the Orbis Terrarum—the populated world that, coincidentally, existed north of the equator. The New World—its encounter and incorporation through the

in which the instinct for nostalgia is absolutely resisted. The nostalgia that the *amereida* denounces is not only nostalgia for what existed in the Americas prior to the encounter with the first Europeans but also nostalgia for a concept of the world that belonged to European culture prior to the appearance of the New World. It is also nostalgia for the unkept promises that European culture had assigned to the New World. Nostalgia is a temptation, "an odor of promises, of clever futures which corrode energy and the effort of an history which has come to mean nothing." Inbred with familiarity and tradition, it blocks the ability to hear and receive the unfamiliar and unknown songs of the Latin American heritage, and it obscures the light of the Latin American atmosphere.

The desire and search for an authentic Latin American existence divested of nostalgia leads to the formulation of questions, in the poem, about the "inheritance": of what does it consist, and what is its origin, not from the Latin perspective, alone, or from the perspective of the indigenous cultures, alone, but from the overlay of these *on the continent*. And, significantly, it introduces the question of, and the need for, a sign of this origin.[52]

•

neither memories, nor climates, nor events which concern us, give meaning to place
because our native soil never was adaptability
beyond the inheritance, the earth emerges when it finds us seated
adversity or fortune are beats of the same heart
where the will risks loyalty or abandonment
obedience or phantom
we are lost in pursuit of our own footsteps—behind the overlight there is always a sign
does it have a sign, our origin? what origin?
presently we dream our origin in a diverse luso-castilian language in countries which do
not begin to be nations—in multiple, even innumerable, races and we call ourselves
americans the presence and the name—this our presence and our name—detaching
itself from Europe
the ancient robbed
we know that histories record, measures confirm
artifice operates
more than poetry
behind all light is a sign which veils and unveils the sense of direction

revised physical and metaphysical vision of the world, its invention, even, came to mean for the Europeans a completion of the concept of the world; a "finishing" of the world to the colonialist mentality in which one finds justification for the physical conquest and appropriation of the newly "discovered" continent and its inhabitants.

50. "Que también para nosotros / el destino despierte mansamente / desde aquello gratuidad del yerro / se abren todavía." Iommi, amereida, 5.

51. "Entre simulacros y fantasmas las gentes de américa sólo imitamos". Ibid., 11.

52. Mario Gongóra, the noted Chilean historian and disciple of O'Gorman, in "una Cultura Americana, Entrevista a Mario Gongóra," Revista Universitaria No. 34 (1991), speaks of the lack of a clear cultural consciousness in Latin America. He maintains that there exists "at least a political-

territorial consciousness" in the creating of nations but suggests that emerging cultural consciousness is associated with the creation or recognition of distinct foundation symbols or signs.

its song is "cifra,"[53]*—instinct and calculation, never sentiment*
in the same mode as apparition and apparitions, not idols and ghosts
reality transparent in its vertigo

who without "cifra" speaks of an origin, since only poetically origin reveals itself?

•

This question of origin, sign, and deciphering sets up the task of *amereida* and, in a corollary manner, has a profound influence on much of the work of the institute, including the Open City of Amereida. It is very important that the sign is related to "cifra," to instinct and calculation that replace the sentiment of nostalgia and, therefore, the previously attended idols and phantoms. It is also critical that "cifra" refers both to poetry and the act of making marks that may be physical in nature—that the sign of origin appears only through poetic activity.

The next pages of the poem *amereida* focus the search for origin and sign. America appeared when Christopher Columbus was looking for something else. "columbus / never came to america / he was looking for the Indies // in the middle of his task / this earth / burst forth as a gift // soon / the gift / surged / contrary to intentions / foreign to the expectation // bringing with it / its donation / its conclusions / its boundaries."[54] The perception of the continent presenting itself to the "discoverers" as a gift is stated in conjunction with the observation that, because the continent was perceived by the Spanish and Portuguese as an obstacle in the path of a western route to the Indies and the promised wealth of the enterprise, it was encountered but not accepted. The poem continues, stating that because it was this enterprise that forced the encounter and the conquering and settling of America by the Europeans, their eyes, veiled by other objectives, were unable to see the gift before them. Thus, in essence, the continent remained undiscovered. Instead of accepting the gift and the responsibility of unveiling—revealing the meaning—of that gift, which is implicit in the acceptance, an invented and imported reality was created in which the continent was characterized as paradise: economically, because of the promise of riches to be extracted from its soil, and philosophically, because of the promise of cultural innocence to be found in the people who populated it—Rousseau's "noble savages."

The conquerors and settlers built their cities at the edges of the continent in close proximity to the sea, their highway, in an urban vision eminently Spanish. This is drawn in the *amereida* on a first map. This map

53. *Cifra is difficult to translate with its connotations intact. It means cipher, numbers in figures, or the actual figure of the number, figure itself with a mathematical connotation, or number with a mysterious connotation. The tension is specifically between the way* the word can oscillate between the mysterious and the rational, and in that oscillation is the implication that cifra is analogous to poetry.

54. *"colón / nunca vino a américa / buscaba las indias // en medio de su afán / esta* tierra / irrumpe en regalo // mero / el regalo / surge // contrariando intentos / ajeno a la esperanza // trae consigo / su donación / sus termino / sus bordes"

Quotations from the amereida are marked with single or double diagonals to represent the spatial arrangement of the lines of poetry on the page. A single diagonal (/) indicates vertical and/or horizontal displacement on the page of the following group of words. A double diagonal (//) indicates a return to the left margin.

presents a figure of the South American continent as a contour of dots inside of which there is nothing. Out of this map is born the thesis of *el mar interior* (the interior sea)—the undiscovered and unconquered lands of the continent, neither accepted nor forgotten, but absent when one inquires about the Latin American destiny. And this "interior sea" dares one to lift its veil through *travesía,* which are not discoveries or inventions but acknowledgments: "how to receive america? // be vigilant / raise the veil / across (a *través*) / —the voice tells us— // *travesía* / which is not discovery or invention / but consent // that one's own sea dares us / arise // in gratitude / or recognition / our own liberty."[55]

The word *travesía,* as it is used here, translates to mean voyage or crossing, but specifically in nautical terms. When crossing the Atlantic Ocean, the navigator lifts his face to the stars and is guided by the sky which is "plotted in figures (*cifra*)." These figures, or constellations, in the northern hemisphere move around the pole star, which is located in Ursa Minor. The first Spanish and Portuguese ships of the enterprise to the Indies crossed the equator and, in so doing, lost the pole star that guarded their travels and discovered, as did the poet Dante when he found himself leaving the northern hemisphere to appear in the other, four stars in the shape of a cross—the pole of the other heavens. The Southern Cross guides and guards the travelers of the southern hemisphere. The poem *amereida* lowers it from the heavens and places it over the South American continent to guide travesías through the interior sea. As a pure figure imposed upon the geographic irregularities of the continent, it designates the cardinal points, and the point of confluence of its axis locates Santa Cruz, in Bolivia, as the poetic capital of South America. It becomes the mark that "unveils the sense of direction," which orients the poetic activity of travesía and reorients the traditional understanding of dominance in a referential system in which north is up. Since the Southern Cross becomes the focusing mark, not the equator or the northern hemisphere, both of which belong to an abstract reference system, it follows that south should be "up"—at the top: "and more than south / is this not our north // and its extreme / summit / will appear / to those who // will remount it for the first time?"[56]

The travesía uses the sky as its eyes and the reversing of the cross on the landscape as its map. As it was from the north to the south that the Spanish conquered America, so it is from the south to the north, guided by the imposition of the Southern Cross on the continent, that the interior sea was, and is, to be discovered, the countries separated by this interior sea rejoined, and their common heritage pursued.

55. "como / recibir américa desvelada? // desvelar / rasgar el velo / a través / -la voz nos dice- // travesía / que no des-cubrimiento o invento / con-sentir // que el mar propio y gratuito nos atraviese / levante // en gratitud / o reconoci-ento / nuestra propia libertad"

56. "y más que sur / ¿no es ella nuestro norte // y su extremo / cumbre / aparecida / a quiénes // por primera vez la remontaron?"

From the poem ameredia, *the thesis of the interior sea*

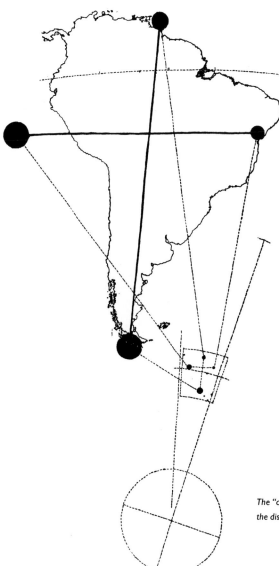

The "cifra" of the Southern Cross laid over the continent to orient
the discovery of the interior sea.

> four stars
>> enfigured
>> like an almond
> they open in their cross
>> all the cardinal points
> the north designates them south
>> but they are not south
> because in this american sky
>> even their light misleads the expectation
>>> - gift or constellation
> to light the map anew
> let us lower their sign over this hour
> introduce their axes
>> into our intimacy
> their spiral
>> onto the interior sea of america
> —Godofredo Iommi

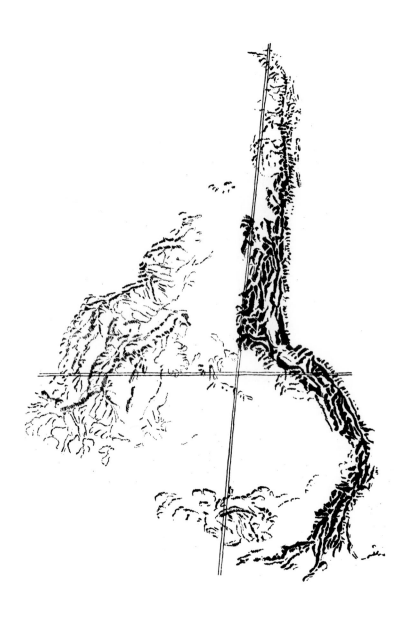

The thesis of the proper north.

and more than south
                    ¿is this not our north
and its extreme
                summit
                        will appear
                                to those who
will remount it for the first time?

The interior sea, both a geographic and a conceptual presence, is not easily known though. It is large and hidden, often appearing as a mirage. It has a dual existence in the poem as both a metaphor for the unencountered Latin American condition and as a concept of a physical place on the continent. It embraces both a physical place and a place in the mind, both of which can be explored and crossed. The physical space of the interior sea can be navigated by car or foot, in travesía, through the figure of the Southern Cross laid on to the continent—cifra as a geometric and cardinal mark—but to navigate the metaphor requires deciphering it through poetic activity, through travesía guided by cifra as poetic marking. Travesía also has a dual existence. It accomplishes a physical crossing and, simultaneously, a mental crossing that is dependent upon language. Language in travesía reconnects the subject to the object—Latin American man to the perception of his physical and cultural heritage—through the mind, whereas the body in travesía reconnects the subject to the object—Latin American man to the South American continent—experientially, *in action.*

"Travesía obtains its sky / like the eyes // its earth thus overcome / is there not exposed in flesh // a rhythm / which moves to language? / because without language // all the routes leading to our intimacy // even though they are taken possession of // deform and deceive // one language?"[57]

Language is the connection to the past through spoken histories. And each of the numerous indigenous languages lives suspended within the Spanish and Portuguese languages that covered the continent. So it is that, parallel to the discovery of the physical continent, there is to occur a discovery of the cultural heritage and its meaning through the map laid down by the numerous languages in which reside the words, the poetry, of the Latin American voice. One voice of numerous languages. To discover this voice is the intention of the activity of the travesía, which uses the Phalène transformed into poetic act.

"In one / leap / we inherited / the other sea / its sky // murders some times // race of races // which language? // light / a gift in travesía / one's amereida // or one's own continent? // let us go"[58]

The *amereida* was written on the eve of the first of many travesías that have been undertaken by the faculty of the Catholic University of Valparaíso.

57. "La travesía consigue su cielo // como los ojos // su tierra así transida / ¿no expondrá en la came // un ritmo / que mueva a lenguaje / porque sin lenguaje // todas las rutas hacia nuestra intimidad // aunque se adueñen // deforman y engañan"

58. "para un / salto / heredamos / otro mar / su cielo // muertos tal vez // raza de razas // ¿cuál lenguaje? // ¿enciende / un regalo en travesía / su amereida // o propio continente? // vamos"

The first travesía, undertaken to engage the interior sea of South America, occurred in August and September of 1965 with a group of ten faculty members of the school: Alberto Cruz, his brother Fabio, Godofredo Iommi and another poet, Claudio Girola and another sculptor, a philosopher, a painter, and two others. It followed the route delineated by the projection of the Southern Cross onto the continental land mass. The goal was to travel from Punta Arenas in the far south of Chile to Santa Cruz de la Sierra in Bolivia: from 52 degrees south of the equator to 18 degrees south. They proclaimed the poetic capital of South America in Santa Cruz de la Sierra, where the prairies stop and the jungle of the Caribbean begins, "the union of the two rhythms of the interior sea of America."[59] Although the final goal of Santa Cruz was stated at the outset, the travesía itself was structureless. Not dissimilar to the surrealist wanderings of Breton and his group, but on a much larger scale, it allowed chance and the spontaneous to intervene in the activity. Intermediate directions and goals were improvised by members of the group, changed or redirected by others. Sometimes two diverging paths were taken concurrently by the splitting of the group. Often the weather and travel conditions were extremely inhospitable, and the last fifty kilometers of the trip were abandoned completely because the road into Santa Cruz was blocked by Ché Guevara's small revolution. The journey or act—the travesía—was made up of numerous poetic acts improvised on sites along the route, and each poetic act left a physical shadow of itself on the site. Something remained whether built, marked, inscribed on, or offered to the site. One returns to cifra not only as the orienting figure but also the physical making of marks. Much of the poem *amereida* discusses the idea of travesía, inventories what will be needed for the first travesía, and relates the idea of travesía to the need for action.

The name "amereida" comes from a joining of America and Eneida (the "Aeneid"), the great mythological foundation epic of Rome composed between 29 and 19 B.C. by the poet Virgil, which describes the wanderings of the Trojan hero Aeneas and a small band of Trojans after the fall of Troy and their adventures upon their arrival in Italy where they become the progenitors of the Roman people. In addition to being the foundation epic of Rome, it is a poem of latinity and of the longing for homeland. Because the Latin condition does not correspond to a nationality—to a place with geographical borders—but rather to a status that is obtained simply by belonging to the world opened by Rome, it is a condition created not by physical limits but by cultural participation in which the Latin language is the binding

59.   "La unión de los dos ritmos del mar interior americano." Godofredo Iommi, amereida volumen segundo (Valparaíso: School of Architecture of the Catholic University of Valparaíso, 1986), 198.

force.[60] In a similar way, the *amereida* wants to uncover the Latin American status that is obtained by belonging to the New World—the gift encountered, but not accepted, by the Latin Europeans. In a certain sense, the first travesía set up by the *amereida* was a symbolic journey of acceptance. Unmistakably associated with the voyages of Ulysses, Aeneas, and Dante, it was more than a journey of discovery. It was an *act* of discovery and consent. The discovery and consent, which is provoked by language in poetic activity, constitutes the acceptance.

But more than this, the amereida travesía was meant to form the foundational sign that the poem *amereida* was searching for: the sign of the Latin American origin. Intended as both a poetic declaration of the concept of "amereida," of Latin America's condition as a gift to the world, and as a course of action to uncover the mystery of this gift, it was clearly a gesture of foundation: symbolically, metaphorically, and actually. Symbolically, the travelers wrote the word amereida on the ground.

•

12 August

At approximately 4 in the afternoon we see a mill near the road. We stop the car. We make our way to it. The pampa is this black region. Mill with watering trough. No one around. Alberto with stones, helped by Jorge, writes on the ground AMEREIDA 1965. Fabio, with a broken piece of the watering trough, erects it and with some stones makes a stele. Tumulus. I climb the mill and lay out some dry branches and Godo catches up with me with some twigs with a little flower or yellow grass. With a piece of wire found there I make a sign and put it in the water pipe which runs from the mill to the water tank. Fedier takes photos. Edy says some words over the place. The cloudy sky and the light suspended in the sunset. We continue the journey. We arrive at Marchand Station. We fill the gas tank.[61]

•

Metaphorically, the amereida travesía *was* the poem *amereida* set on the ground walking, a transfer from mental space to physical space and extended half the length of the continent. It also was a gesture that initiated the *doing* of travesía, thereby laying the foundation for all subsequent travesías as an active and vital way of working related to (re)search of origin.

In a sense then, the poem *amereida* fulfills itself. It turns a circle in on itself but without closing it. It asks for sign of origin and it creates this sign of origin: the amereida travesía. But the sign is illusive. It is not physical but a course of action. It is clear that the *amereida* does not recreate the founda-

60. Pérez-Oyarzún, "The Valparaíso School," 90.

61. Iommi, amereida volumen segundo, 170.

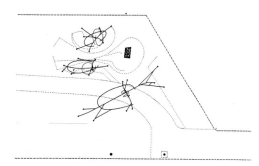

A travesía beside the Mapocho River in Santiago entitled Athenea.
The poem by Godofredo Iommi is engraved on the solid sculpture.
(UCV archives)

Athenea

    Cual promisorio
        o detrás
    cercado luz
    - el secreto no registra -
Aún otra
    íntima
se dice a si
conmoviendo la aparencia
Tal antaño
        por nieves negras
al hilo
    ciñe
        ciegas
          libertades
            recurrentes
Esta tierra guarda
el silencio inviolable de su eco
y vedada
se enamora de sus gentes
    Lámpara
        que todo olvido vuelve.

Athenea

    As promising
        or behind
    enclosed light
    —the secret does not register—
Even another
    intimates
says to herself
stirring her appearance
As before
        by black snows
watchful
    she girds
        blind women
          recurrent
            liberties
This land keeps
the inviolable silence of its echo
and forbidden
it falls in love with its people
    Lamp
        that every oblivion returns.

tion of Latin American culture. It does, however, create the foundation for a critical understanding of that culture and for the metamorphosis of a sensibility with regard to that culture and, very importantly, it creates the foundation for an authentic and original form of historical and cultural research that absolutely relies on action in addition to speculation. Finally, it also creates the foundation for a way of researching and acting within the natural context of the South American continent.

7 *Travesía inunda el continente y el mundo / andar cantando / juego de niños*[62]

Since the first travesía, the amereida travesía, the concept of travesía has proven to be of immense value to the research of the institute. So much so that in the early 1980s it became a part of the pedagogical program in which the third trimester of each year is reserved for research in travesía with students and professors. The pedagogic travesías have altered slightly the physical concept of crossing. The first travesía (crossing) was conceived as a wandering directed by the geometric imposition of the Southern Cross on the continent, whereas now the pedagogic travesía are journeys undertaken to remote, but predetermined, sites of South America. Although spatially altered, they still remain loyal to the concept of a journey that changes the meaning of things through poetry. They still respond to the original passion for doing as well as to the metaphorical concept of crossing. The crossing is not intended as a means to arrive at another place but rather as an experience that changes the perceived meaning of things: "The voyages teach us (among other things) that words are foreign to the things they designate."[63] They effect a mental crossing from a conventional understanding of reality to another understanding of reality in which language opens up reality to its meaning, its profound meaning discovered through poetic correspondences of conventionally unrelated phenomena.

As an extension and prolongation of the original journey of discovery, the travesías that have since occurred have proven to serve two purposes. First, to discover the power and value of the natural continent in relationship to a concept of history in which the Latin American heritage is considered a gift and, second, to inform the way of doing/making through the discovery. Like the wanderings of the surrealist poets, the travesías probe the boundaries between rationalized experience and intuitive discovery and, through this probing, begin a process of initiation, of beginning. This is the important

62. "Travesía floods the continent and the world / to go (walk, travel) singing / a game of children," Alberto Cruz, in notes taken from a lecture at the Catholic University of Valparaíso, July 1992.

63. "Los viajes nos enseñan (entre otras cosas) que las palabras son como extrañas a las cosas que nombran." Iommi, amereida, 77.

A travesía entitled "Ulises," constructed in Pisagua, a ghost port in the northern desert.
The poem is inscribed on the hanging panels.

Ulises

Un huésped es un héroe que regresa de la guerra en que
    encumbró su nombre
Un huésped es un rey que va hacia la casa que dejó sin cuerpo
Un huésped es un jefe que ha perdido la mesnada con que se
    haría dueño
Un huésped es un nadie que tropieza la mar de veces con los
    dioses
Un huésped es un solitario que cruza umbrales donde hay
    desiertos
Un huésped es un novio dado de lado por la virgen de la distancia
Un huésped es un sacerdote que celebra el sacrificio de la pasada
Un huésped es un amante que aprende que son las diosas las
    fugaces
Un huésped es un rehén que compra su libertad con su cuento
Un huésped es un poeta que encuentra sus palabras con sus
    pasos
Un huésped es un lenguaraz que larga los secretos que apartan
    las lenguas
Un huésped es un importuno que al llegar hace ver que él era el
    esperado
Un huésped es un mendigo que declina la corona porque va con el
    trono
Un huésped es un deudo cuya sangre es igual a la tuya pero
    oreada
Un huésped es un ebrio que recuerda más hechos que los que
    comprende el vino
Un huésped es un comensal que sazona golosinas con lágrimas
Un huésped es un seductor que obtiene que los celos le allanen la
    marcha
Un huésped es un ladrón que se lleva el albergue y deja los trastos
Un huésped es un vago que amenaza la fundación estanca de los
    mundos
Un huésped es un esposo que tarda hasta que su mujer se vuelve
    enigma
Un huésped es un padre cuyo hijo lo busca donde no puede
    encontrarlo
Un huésped es un hombre que invita a hablar todavía a los
    muertos
Un huésped es un agente que guarda en su cuerpo el final del
    canto

Ulises

A huésped* is a hero who returns from a war in which he exalted
    his name
A huésped is a king who goes to the house which he left without
    body
A huésped is a chief who has lost the soldiers with which he would
    have become master
A huésped is a nobody who sometimes skips over the sea with the
    gods
A huésped is a lonely man who crosses thresholds where there are
    deserts
A huésped is a bridegroom given from the side of the virgin of
    distance
A huésped is a priest who celebrates the sacrifice of the past
A huésped is a lover who learns that the goddesses are the
    fugitives
A huésped is a hostage who buys his liberty with his story
A huésped is a poet who finds his words with his footsteps
A huésped is a talkative man who loosens the secrets which
    languages separate
A huésped is an inopportune man who at his arrival makes it
    seem that he was expected
A huésped is a beggar who declines the crown because it comes
    with a throne
A huésped is a relative whose blood is the same as yours but with
    fresh air
A huésped is a drunk who remembers more deeds than those
    which wine is made of
A huésped is a fellow diner who seasons his delicacies (longings)
    with tears
A huésped is a seductor who obtains that jealousies smooth the
    march for him
A huésped is a thief who steals the inn but leaves behind the
    useless utensils
A huésped is a vagabond who menaces the immovable foundation
    of the world
A huésped is a husband who delays until his wife becomes an
    enigma
A huésped is a father who searches for his son where he can not
    find him
A huésped is a man who still invites the murdered to speak
A huésped is an agent who keeps in his body the end of the song.

*Huésped does not translate with its full meaning intact. Literally
    it is a guest or lodger but with the implication of one who is a
    recurrent traveler, perhaps even a wanderer.

contribution of the concept of travesía to the work of the Catholic University of Valparaíso: the initiation of a physical material work on the site, whether it be a relatively insignificant mark or gesture, as was more typical of the first travesía, or a more ambitious "project," as is often the experience of the more recent travesías. The travesía provokes the interpretation of the space of the site through words and language and then, through words and language, it constructs space within the site. It unites the processes of interpretation and transformation.

The built part of the travesías have taken many forms and scales: pavilion-sized sculptures, a forest of wind pipes in the highlands of Patagonia, a built line running for several kilometers across the floor of a volcanic valley in the Atacama desert, small theater pieces, a prototypical boat intended to navigate the southern fjordal region of Chile—a form of urbanism of the sea. The amereida travesía was significant in that it engaged space half the length of the continent, and it built its mark the corresponding length, while the more recent travesías are more punctual. The marks and projects, once made, are abandoned to the elements and to their own uncertain futures. They become offerings or gifts returned to the site. The main impetus for the making is the making itself.

The concept of travesía engages space, place, and poetry through improvisational activity. In this sense it is not dissimilar to the phalène established at the beginning of the research activities of the institute. In fact, it is clear that the travesía is an extension of the idea of the original phalène to a larger context. It is, however, in its extension that the travesía sets up the possibility of *building space* that originates in the poetic word and, therefore, is essential to the conception of the Open City. The phalène began as a recitation of poetry in group to a group. It therefore began to engage space physically by the quantity and configuration of the people performing and participating. The phalènes were most often done in public spaces, and there was a consequent relationship between the place of their recitation and the content of the poetry. As it developed into a making of poetry, the relationship between language and place began to uncover the meaning of place through the coincidental relationship of site and language. However, space still remained a suggestion dependent upon the physical performancelike aspect of the act. The phalène suggests space through the gesture of recitation (or making) of poetry. The poetic acts of the travesía engage space through the primary gesture of marking with poetry, serving to discover the phenomenological meanings inherent in the site and translate these meanings to the

The road to the Casa de los Nombres under construction

construction of space that marks the site. Implicit in marking is the idea that one merely chooses a portion of the space of the site to hold, articulate, or delineate in physical construction; that the physical construction is not a foreign imposition of built space—rather, that the "act of building is light."[64] In the phalène, poetry operates in recitation and remains in the realm of language; whereas in the travesía, poetry operates as incantation to create a "communicating vessel" between language and space.

palabras acaban
palabras comienzan
encierran
liberan
destruidas en tedios
renovadas en necesidades
vidas son sacrificadas a palabras
palabras son sacrificadas a vidas[65]

Specifically from the proposition of travesía—of creating something on the site, of the site, in a poetic way of doing—one finds in the poem *amereida* the articulation of several interrelated ideas that provoke the conception of the Open City Amereida in Ritoque. The ideas include concepts of imaginary cities, or a single imaginary city, thoughts about the tradition of agora as the intersection of public man and natural site, thoughts about the laws of nature as traditionally related to the process of building in the "innocence of an archaism," and speculations about building on an earth in which the "act of building is light"—of little consequence. In its specificity, the *amereida* can be seen as a charter for the Open City. However, unlike traditional charters it does not lay down structures and laws but instead establishes the foundation for a way of acting. It is the concept of travesía invented by the *amereida* that bridges theoretical speculation relative to this way of acting and concrete action necessary to the making of the Open City.

In essence the work at the Open City has been done as in travesía. Like the first travesía, the amereida travesía, there are certain parameters that loosely structure the improvisational making and marking of space in an extended natural site. Also, like the amereida travesía, there is an element of wandering attached to a crossing or voyage. However, whereas the wandering of the amereida travesía was attached to a theoretically constructed geometric projection that extended half the continent and occurred over

64.   *Ibid.*

65.   "words conclude / words begin / enclose / liberate / destroyed by boredom / renewed by need / lives are sacrificed to words / words are sacrificed to lives," *Ibid.,* 74.

The Music Room in the dunes of the Open City

several months, at the Open City of Amereida the wandering is across and through the territory defined by the boundaries of ownership of the site; it constantly folds back on itself and has been occurring for over twenty-five years. At the Open City, the train and its track that cross the site metaphorically replace the original idea of voyage as something projected from one point in place and time to another point in place and time, while the actual travesía crossing is again and again across the site along different trajectories with different characteristics.

Although the Catholic University of Valparaíso was founded in 1952, it was not until March 1970 that the Open City was begun: eighteen years of experimentation and vigil in which the founding attitudes related to the centering of architecture in the poetic word were at work. It is through travesía that much of the teaching and experimentation is now focused, and it is through the idea/attitude/method of travesía that the Open City has achieved material significance.

If *travesía* can be loosely defined as a journey in which discovery and improvisation attached to language in poetic activity produce a certain mental crossing, and if the Open City can be understood as having been mentally and physically constructed as in travesía, then perhaps some of the results come into sharper focus. From the initial founding of the Open City when the site was opened by a poetic act in which the concept of the "volver a no saber" was discovered in the sand, an urban legacy was initiated in which discovery and improvisation attached to language in poetic activity, the poetic act, take precedence over imposed formal ordering systems or functional pre-occupations.[66] Each time a new work is begun at the Open City, the site is rediscovered through poetic act, and from these acts, building is initiated.

Poetic acts are used to discover sites of construction, and they are used to discover strategies for the making of space. Depending upon the complexity of the proposed project or the length of its construction time, these may or may not occur simultaneously, or there may be a series of poetic acts that occur at different stages of the conception and design of the project. Once the initial discovery/design of the project has taken place, the work progresses accordingly. In some cases, this means that work is done as a complex collaboration between professors and students, each contributing tactics and design ideas. In other cases, one or more individuals may lead portions of the work. This can be seen in the relative aspects of the structures: those that are more aggregative versus those that are more autonomous. Building is done by the professors and students *en rondo* (in teams) in conjunction with

66.   *From the beginning, the poetic act has been the component of the travesía in which poetry is engaged. Travesía is a concept of journey and crossing that includes the poetic act as its tool.*

Out in the dunes of the Open City, the Music Room is located in a
sheltered hollow. It is a rectangular white building specifically conceived for the performance of modern music. Its corners are
broken open for entry, support functions, and light. Penetrating
vertically through the center of the box is a volume of natural light
approximately five feet square, defined by a set of four triple-hung
windows that enable the vertical space to be completely opened
or closed. This volume of light funnels the atmospheric conditions
of the exterior, which change with the time of day, year, or the
weather, into the interior of the building. Due to its placement the

musician(s) can not occupy the center of the room and are instead dislodged to the side. To compensate for and make use of the off-centering of the music in the space, the interior walls were built as vertical panels attached to the walls by tracks, which enables them to be pulled out from the walls, turned, and angled to use either a bamboo-covered side that is acoustically absorptive or the other side that is acoustically reflective. Additionally, the ceiling of the space folds down into a series of planes that serve to focus the sound outward and around the light pillar. In this way the entire room can be literally tuned to the placement and ear of the musi-cian and audience. The displacement of the musician by light and conversion of the entire room into a sounding box creates an experience of the harmonies and dissonances of the properties and phenomena associated with light and sound. Within the box, one is enveloped by the two phenomena as presences in the space, whether music is being played or not. When players are absent, the sea's sound enters through the central light box, and music is made with the voice and the light of the sea. A simile is created with the way in which, outside, the rhythm of the sea and the sun operate upon the space of the site.

Two studio buildings sit adjacent to each other among the rolling dunes opposite the Hospedería de los Diseños. The first one to be built was a workshop designed to accommodate the building of small- to medium-scale projects. Space was discovered between a plane rising out of the crest of the dunes and the fall of the sand leeward to a lower ground level. The upper surface of the plane is set with paving stones to create an informal plaza and outdoor discussion space. It reaches out to the city of Valparaíso, standing in as foreground and reminding one of the relative understanding of "ground plane" with regard to the position of the eye, and it displays the simplicity with which one can discover and construct space in the primitive gesture of delaminating the surface of the ground.

The second workshop building is a rectangular box sitting between two square exterior courts, one on its south side and one on its north side. The building volume, because of its proportions and orientation, splits the sun's illumination into light and shadow so that one of the courts is almost always in light and the other one is almost always in shadow. The roof of the building is transparent plastic; in essence there is no roof, only a presence of ambient light. Windows at the ground level band the building, allowing views into both courts while emphasizing the horizon line through parallelism and creating a sensation of the volume of the build-

ing floating just above eye level. Two large doors centered on the longer sides of the building open to allow the passage of large sculpture and construction pieces into, out of, or through the building, facilitated by a large wooden trussed frame extending through the building into both courts. The truss allows for the manipulation of the objects so that they may be worked on under three precise conditions: in intense natural light, in muted ambient light, or in shadow. Succinctly, the building is a filter that separates out these three conditions.

Across the highway from the coastal dunes is a steep cliff face that rises to the upper plateau of the Open City. On the upper plateau, which is a fertile plane of grasses, deciduous and evergreen trees, a palace and cemetery have been built along with several hospederías, an agora, and a sun garden. The Engineer's House was built at the edge of this plateau. Although situated overlooking the sea, the house visually turns its back on the sea (see also top figure, p. 22). A series of five and a half hexagons creates the spatial structure of the house, which turns around an inner court through

which one enters the house—a spiral within a spiral. Its geometry creates a series of facets that diffuse the panoramic view, allowing for openings that do not turn out to the sea but back toward the mountains and across the upper plateau. The geometrical order of the house is apparent from the air but less apparent from the ground because it is intended as a structure that is very "light handed," permitting the gestures of the house—relative to the landscape or to interior activities—to override. Just as the facets of the hexagons are used to diffuse the traditional panoramic

view, the improvisational and idiosyncratic insertion of windows, masonry surfaces, metal panels, light boxes, folded plates, and so forth diffuse the geometrical order. The roof plane, which belies the order, viewed from the approach attaches itself to the space of the site as it mimics the silhouette of Valparaíso in the distance, or as a reminder of the great sailing vessels that traversed this coast, and the furling of their sails as they put into port or departed out to sea.

The Engineer's House

Another hospederia on the high ground

Detail of fanning sunscreen on the face of the hospedería which opens to the water. In the background is the palace.

Situated further back on the plateau is the Hospederia del Er-
rante, which is unfinished and abandoned at this time. Yet even as
a ruin its intentions are clear as it opens up toward the mountains
with an entry ramp and an unfolded corner that frames the folded
forms of the mountains in the distance. An atrium space, which
the ramp accesses at the upper level, turns toward the tree line,
allowing the impact of the mountains in the landscape to be de-
coded through their memory uncluttered by their visual presence.

contractors. In general, the students' work is enlisted for projects that require large amounts of physical labor, such as the roads, or projects and portions of projects on a smaller scale that require a certain precision and finesse. If a project incorporates scavenged material such as windows from demolished buildings, this material becomes an essential element within the design strategy and development. Construction documents are not made, and each project progresses at its own pace. Since all funding is provided by the faculty of Architecture, there are no outside pressures to force an imposed schedule. There is, moreover, no clear definition or sacredness to the end of the building process. Some structures never "finish," and all of them are capable of accepting additions and transformations.

At the Open City, loyalty to the concept of discovery relative to the positioning of construction on the site has led to a construction of city in which ad-hocism has superseded the imposition of plan. Loyalty to the concept of discovery relative to spatial strategies of individual projects has led to a series of constructions in which the subject matter of each construction, the meaning, is integrally related to the act of discovery and its particular experience and perception of the site. Therefore, inherent in the meaning of many of the projects is a reference or relationship to the initial act from which the project was conceived. That the discovery is made through language in poetic activity, and specifically activity that attempts to activate the more mysterious regions of thought enlisting chance in the process, means that the results, both on the urban scale and on the scale of individual projects, are unpredictable.

ahora está el lugar para poetrías ni hipnotizantes ni consoladores
poetrías que transforman cada momento al tacto
en nuevos momentos de nuevas poetrías[67]

Poetic acts function through improvisation. Implicit within the word *improvise* is the recognition of a base of material with which—or out or which— one constructs in an unprovided, unforeseen, unpredictable, provisional way. Music that is improvisational works off of a foundation of notes and their geometric interrelationships, tone, beat, compositional knowledge, and so on. Improvisational theater works from a series of first assumptions about characteristics and personality traits of the players, the basic scenario and time frame for the piece, with the results being completely left open to unfold as they will. The foundation of material for the work of the Open City comprises,

67. *"now is the place for poetry not hypnotizers nor comforters / poetries which transform each moment into the tactile / in new moments of new poetries,"* lommi, amereida, 74.

among other things, a certain base of knowledge with regard to the interrelationship of space and phenomena as they exist and present themselves within the physical context in which the Catholic University of Valparaíso works. This base of knowledge, however, is something that has been generated through discovery and which becomes an intuitive understanding transformed by individual experience and interpretation. It is knowledge as memory, easily accessible to the imagination.

This memory exists on several levels: memory related to the physical context, to the mental site, and to the physical act of building things with one's own body. As an intuitive knowledge base, it transforms through improvisation to become part of the illusive thematic base underlying the work of the Open City.

Memory related to the physical context of the work of the Catholic University of Valparaíso includes, certainly, the city of Valparaíso, but it also includes the regions of the continent crossed by travesías. The travesías expand the physical space of the work so that the physical context is never approached through specificities of location (*genus loci*) but through its interconnectedness within the larger landscape of the continent. Physical context is not about the fragmentation of space but the reconnection of space through the correspondences between things and phenomena; it is about the unity, the homogeneity, of space, not focused upon individual disconnected parts and pieces. For this understanding, the travesías are of vital importance.

Memory related to the mental site of the work of the Catholic University of Valparaíso has evolved through poetry and is accessed by the poetic act. It is attached to the history and heritage of the Latin American continent as proposed by the poem *amereida* and by subsequent poetic work that has transformed the original mental site. It was modern French poetry that opened this mental site, which focuses on the Latin American condition while it, simultaneously, inserted into the site another body of subject matter related to the human condition in the modern world of ideas. Because this knowledge is not founded only on research of physical space but space inhabited by language and the mind, it is very illusive and capable of its own transformation and mutation.

Memory related to the physical act of building things is constructed out of the doing of things, of building things on the sites of travesías. It is related to the processes of construction and related to an attitude toward building. As has been stated, the work of the Open City accepts that construction is going to be mostly artisanal. Therefore the materials used are those that can be moved and put together by hand or light machinery—wood, brick, some precast concrete, sheet metal, cloth, plastics—and the construction methods are those related to these materials. The result when an improvisational way of working is applied to these materials and construction methods is a type of construction that is light on and in the landscape, both physically and conceptually.

In service of the improvisational workings of the poetic act, this intuitive knowledge base transforms to become part of the illusive thematic base underlying the work of the Open City. When applied to an attitude toward the building process, a process that clearly accepts the improvisational and provisional, the forms and materiality of the built work begin to reveal their own process of coming to be and an architectural language of improvisation develops. In a sense, like the modern French poets who sought to create a language that was more consequent with the subject matter arising from unknown regions of the mind, the work of the institute has discovered its own architectural language that has arisen from this attitude toward the improvisational and provisional and is, therefore, more consequent to its subject matter. It is a language that has developed from the process of thinking and propositioning the act of making architecture in relationship to a poetic base and attitude. It is capable of expressing this relationship and, in many cases, the act of propositioning as well. At the Open City the formal languages of the structures such as the Music Pavilion, workshops, and Hospedería La Alcoba result from the relationship of tectonics to poetic ideation; the subject matter is in the idea and the idea is articulated in the tectonics. In the more aggregative structures, epitomized by the double hospedería, the poetic ideas are spoken about in the tectonics and in the formal language, but the propositioning of the *act of making* becomes the true subject. Also in the palace in the highlands—because the form and space was set at the moment, and by the moment, in which it was declared set—the building becomes the manifestation of the architectural proposition. The moment set in form. And the architectural language used becomes liberated to exist as its own entity.

Because it is a language that derives from the process of propositioning architecture, it is a language that, itself, is up for discussion. It is continually being reinvented. It is not intended to give lectures on style or form or to be evocative. It is open. And because it is a language that is capable of expressing the architect's process of making propositions about space and a consequent way of acting and constructing that space, it is a language

Casa Cruz, Santiago, 1991

that may be that "suggestive magic containing at the same time the object and the subject, the world exterior to the artist and the artist himself." [68]

One of the first confrontations of major significance between the making of architectural form and the propositioning of the architectural process with reference to this material base is found in a house built by Fabio Cruz in Santiago for his father, a retired General of the Chilean Army. It is a seminal work and a critical precedent for the work to follow at the Open City. Until the summer of 1992, when it was demolished in preparation for the construction of a high-rise apartment building, its physical reality, which was very significantly determined by the story of its materialization, demonstrated that a fusion was conceivable between form/language and the poetic process of architectural proposition. Now, as a memory, it remains as a suggestion and not a demonstration.

The Cruz house was begun in 1959 on a tight suburban site 53 feet wide and 100 feet deep. The house, surrounded completely by traditional houses, did not pretend to accommodate its neighbors but instead developed in deference to its own ambitions. It is constructed around a structure of reinforced concrete columns and beams that was built first as the only fixed element of the house. Because the project was to begin with the construction of the concrete portions, the City permitted the work to commence with only approved structural plans. This set the precedent for the remaining construction, which advanced in an ad-hoc manner but was guided by an architectural-spatial concept: the desire to confuse the boundary between the house—its spaces and surfaces—and the ground, and to mix its spatial volume with the sky. The spatial covering developed not as a continuous covering but one that breaks and folds up into different planes with different forms that leave hollows of the sky among them. The planes gather the changing light and shadow, and the windows among them orient the passage of the sky from one side to another. Originally the windows were planned as part of the facade design, but as the work progressed the windows appeared to take matters into their own hands and the views, framing, quality of light and air movement began to determine sizes, forms, locations, which of the windows or wall panels opened. Small windows became whole panels of glass. Transparent glass became translucent. One window was particularly disobedient; as the builders hoisted it into place, it slipped to hang by its corner and was built into the wall in that position. "Chance liberates the hands always tied by that which is known." [69]

68.   "une magie suggestive contenant à la fois l'objet et le sujet, le monde extérieur à l'artiste et l'artiste lui-même." Charles Baudelaire, as cited by William Rees, French Poetry 1820–1950 (London: Penguin Books, 1990), 135.

69.   Alex Moreno, "Casa Cruz, Comentario a la obra," ARQ 16 (March 1991): 39.

The work progressed step by step without definitive or complete plans, learning from the site itself. It was invented as it needed to be. The only fixed plans were those for the structural concrete that determined the volume and geometry of the house. The geometry derives from the triangulation of a square, with the intention of engaging and expanding the entire site and its natural elements from the interior space, through the diagonal. The geometrical preoccupation exists as a remnant of the mathematics that Alberto Cruz wanted to extract architecture from, but in this instance the geometry does not articulate the space but exists as one element of it and, in some cases, is completely disregarded by it.

There is much more to say about the Casa Cruz, about its materiality, about architectural detail, about the dematerialization of surface and volume, about the light, about the way its space folds, about its sense of humor. Of greater significance to this discussion, however, is its seminal role within the work of the institute. That it conceived the foundation of a language consequent with its subject matter and the propositioning of the architectural process. That this language is a language of improvisation.

The architectural language of the Casa Cruz began its flirtation with the improvisational at the moment in which it was decided that no building plans were to be made. Instead a spatial strategy as a geometrical apparatus was devised/designed/divined to organize the house through the diagonal in order to create an expanded set of oblique relationships between the interior spaces and the site. The spatial strategy committed itself to a physical framework with which the phenomena of the site interacted. This physical framework was set down in the triangulated concrete structure of the building and in the split and triangulated sections of the roof. Inside this spatial strategy, design continued tactically. Design tactics were revised, changed, and redirected as information about the site and its phenomena—the movement of the natural light, the wind, the rain—intervened, and as the actual process of construction intervened. The architect participated simultaneously in the design and construction of the house and on the site of construction, becoming, in a certain sense, a medium through which the phenomena of the site and the process of construction were interpreted in the design tactics. In this way, an immediate relationship between the site, the process of construction, and the project was created.

At the Open City, the first buildings, the hospederías, developed in a similar way to the Casa Cruz with the difference being that the architect as medium was replaced by poetry as medium with the group of architects, poets, sculptors, and engineers as its vehicle. Poetry as an instrument of discovery in travesía—creates a similar architectural language to that used in the Casa Cruz but with syntactical results that are less predictable. Within this group of hospederías, the anomaly is the Banquet Hospedería. In this project, reliance on spatial strategy has been discarded so that design activity is produced as an accretion of tactics informed by poetry. It is interesting that this project is the one that has been added to and reworked most often. It is probably fair to say that its language stretches to the limits the improvisational and provisional at the Open City.

At the Open City as well, the natural site is more complex than the site of the Casa Cruz in Santiago, and even this site in Ritoque has been significantly expanded through travesía. Therefore, the language that is partially derived from its relationship to site transforms to admit this complexity and expansion. The site as a seam between sea and land has varied and distinct characteristics. Some of the projects are conceived and built in the transitional dunes, which are somewhat more stable than the sand dunes as they are capable of supporting vegetation; some are built on the high grass plateau overlooking the dunes, and the Casa de los Nombres is built in the coastal sand dunes. The distinct characteristics from one part of the site to the other elicit different transformations and permutations of meaning, materiality, construction methods, and language. The Casa de los Nombres, as the last project built to date and the only project built in the expanse of the sand dunes, was an attempt to construct or mark space in the most fluid and instable part of the site—neither sand nor sea yet simultaneously sand and sea, which move with the wind. Structural challenges presented by the site, their spatial implications, and the dialogue with meaning clearly required a rediscovery and improvisational application of materiality, construction methods, and therefore language. It is a building that is similar to some of the others in language and thematics while being completely unlike any of the others in the way it makes legible the fluidity of the wind and the dunes.

The challenge of building in the dunes and the meaning engaged by that challenge, as seen in the Casa de los Nombres, occurred through the concept of travesía, which allows, in fact requires, that each building site at the Open City be seen as a completely new site—a new journey and new crossing—while simultaneously belonging to the unity of the landscape and its phenomena. This promotes a physical presence in which buildings in close proximity to each other have certain *correspondences* of meaning and language while denying formal and spatial interrelationships. The Open City

defers to the individual improvisational relationships made by each project with their physical and mental sites, creating a city in which mental correspondences have replaced physical ordering structures. "The relationships between places and buildings are none other than those of being travesías in the way of Amereida."[70]

8 *Je suis un éphémère et point trop mécontent citoyen d'une métropole crue moderne, parce que tout goût connu a été éludé dans les ameublements et l'extérieur des maisons aussi bien que dans le plan de la ville. Ici vous ne signaleriez les traces d'aucun monument de superstition. La morale et la langue sont réduites à leur plus simple expression, enfin!*[71]

Without the urban imprint of a city plan, without the physical aspect of city—roads, streets, density, fabric—and without the inclusive accommodation of all aspects of daily communal life—there are no schools or churches, commerce does not exist, and daily articles of consummation are brought from the outside—one has to wonder what it is that makes the Open City of Amereida a city. Is it a city? Or, given its relationship to the pedagogical agenda of the Institute for Architecture, which insists on the transformation of study into creative research—the merging of art and life so that life becomes a laboratory for the imagination—is the Open City a laboratory: a laboratory of urban settlement? In the sand, in what was originally zoned as coastal park, there is something occurring that is not recreational in intent but instead is about civil work. It certainly could be considered a laboratory in that the work is research oriented—not dependent on clients and commissions. But it also has a physical consequence and communal framework that transgress the boundary between research and practice. From either position, as city or as laboratory, what is significant is that the Open City poses fundamental questions as to what constitutes "city" and urbanism.

Certainly no city has ever appeared overnight with all of its physical characteristics intact. However, it is possible to affirm that a city has its character predetermined from the moment of its founding. In Latin America this idea is especially relevant as the cities of the Spanish conquest and settlement were conceived intact. It was a vision of city ordered and structured for settlement. For the establishment and exposition of the seat of power: the *plaza mayor*, a collector around which the church and government buildings were organized. For the acquisition and efficient control of land: the grid that was laid over the land often regardless of previous construction and only adapting

70. "Las relaciones entre los lugares y edificios no son otras que aquellas de ser travesías al modo de Amereida," Godofredo Iommi and Alberto Cruz, "la ciudad abierta: de la utopía al espejismo," Revista Universitaria 9, 23.

71. "I am an ephemeral and a not too discontented citizen of a metropolis considered modern, because all known taste has been eluded in the furnishings and the exterior of the houses as well as in the plan of the city. Here you will not find the trace of a single monument to superstition. Morality and language are reduced to their simplest expression, at last!" Arthur Rimbaud, "Ville," Les Illuminations (Paris: Mermod, 1962), 48.

El Palacio del Alba y del Ocaso (the Palace of Dawn and Dusk) was designed to be an expansive roofed building, a major place of congregation with spatial relationships to the sunrise and sunset and their respective qualities of light. Formed by unbuttressed brick walls built in bowed segments for lateral stability, it was to have tapestries dividing the spaces. However, when the walls were built to approximately five and a half feet in height, one of the founders, the poet Godofredo Iommi, appeared on the site and declared that the palace was finished. As it stands, it is a series of spaces roofed by the sky and defined by the rhythmic brick walls upon which the sun acts to dematerialize and rematerialize the surface, its mass, and volumes. Exposed to the elements, the floor of the palace is marked with water channels and surface elements that channel and fracture the rainfall; large channels and pools at the entry create the semblance of a moat. The height of the walls, as built, creates a strong horizontal line parallel to the horizon line and just above eye height. An experience is thus created in which the horizon line demarcating the boundary between sea and sky to the topography where it was impossible not to do so. And, for settlement and repayment of loyalty to Spanish citizens: the subdivision of the block formed by the grid into parcels of land as commodities. This vision of the city, which was officially recognized as a model by Felipe II in his Ordinances, set the form of the city and any subsequent growth from the moment of its founding. Its destiny was predetermined by the founding, which consisted of the self-conscious application of the imported Spanish model.

Just as Latin America was an invention and a coming to terms with the piece of land that interrupted Columbus's westward route to the Indies, which necessitated a significant revision of the existing Latin world concept, the Spanish and Portuguese cities founded in the New World were also inventions. They were not formed from morphological growth. They were new, begun from nothing but the idea of settlement, and settlement *for* Spain, at whatever the cost. They represented Spain, and the model itself became a significant symbol of Spain's position within the New World concept. Latin America was founded as a European idea, and the cities were founded relative and relevant to that idea. Their act of founding then becomes both a pragmatic and a symbolic act. It begins, it initiates city. And it is the sign of city: the gesture that sets in motion the idea and destiny of the city within the space.

In Ritoque, at the Open City, the project of building city is also very much attached to this attitude that a city is inherent in its founding because the founding sets in motion the city's destiny. However, unlike the Spanish model, the destiny is not one *formally* predetermined, intact, with all of its infrastructure and building types in place, but is instead open.

In 1953, prior to the founding of the Open City itself, the members of the Catholic University of Valparaíso did a project for an urban settlement of 50,000 workers in Archupallas, which is relevant to this discussion and also to an understanding of the critical context invented by the school relative to urbanism.[72] Seven kilometers north of Valparaíso, Archupallas is a site in the forested hills overlooking the coastal amphitheater of Viña del Mar. The project, which is composed of two parts, a theoretical foundation and a practical proposition, begins with the rejection of conventional planning methodologies, in this case the application of the modernist *cité jardin* as promoted by the developers of the project. Although not opposed to the focus of the project—city toward garden—the members of the Valparaíso school questioned what an application of the model would attain. Suppose that one

72. Alberto Cruz, Godofredo Iommi, Oscar Buttazoni, Manuel Casanueva, Claudio Diaz, Jorge Sanchez, and Juan Verchueren.

laces through the openings between the walls of the palace, merging the space of the palace with the sea and the sky—through the eye. It is also through the eye that the space of the palace is linked to the space and time of the site. Because the palace and its significance were defined by the moment when the founding poet declared the palace done, the physical object contains within it the gesture and the moment of its appearance, of its coming to be, and it contains the significance and purity of the architectural intention materialized in that gesture. It is a building about time in

many aspects: time frozen in the instant of the architectural proposition; the continuum of time as witnessed in the phenomena of the sky; the cycles of time as witnessed in the phenomena of the sky; the separation of time into its two faces of night and day, specifically highlighting the moments of transition at dawn and dusk when the merging and separation of day and night are experienced through the phenomena of light. And it is a building about the vastness of the sky whether crossed by the sun or by the figures of the stars.

could form a garden perfectly urbanized and planned with its architecture and organization set into the amenities of the natural site: the sea, the trees, the earth, the sky. All would be very livable, but what have you really gained beyond an efficient organization and distribution of these natural amenities? Implicit in the question is a rejection of city as the spatial manifestation of an imposed order and efficiency and, as a corollary, a rejection of plan making as the expediter of this imposed order that fixes and closes the possibility of city because it does not provide space for those intangible things of human-urban correspondence.

Rejection of plan making, by association, places in question the role of the urbanist. If it is not to make plans, then what?: "Is this (plan making) the work of the urbanist, his only enterprise? No. The urbanist discovers the destiny of the city and positions it in the space so that the city and its inhabitants live their destiny—be it gentle or hard, heroic or nonheroic."[73] The urbanist as plan maker is replaced by the urbanist as medium whose task is to set in motion the destiny of the city. And, very clearly, the urbanist is the architect because it is the "architect (who) sings about daily life." The city is the architect's work. The architect understands space and spaces—plazas, streets, and so on—as they relate to urban life, its phenomena and its structure, qualitatively; whereas the planner deals with it quantitatively, organizing and distributing it, subjecting it to patterns. The city is life, changing and re-forming. It is not the organization of urban elements because "organization only makes a place for itself and for its systems of organization to exist."[74] It does not provide for, or fulfill, the complexities of the city as a living organism that houses the spontaneity of its population in civic body.

"The urbanist discovers the *destiny* of the city and positions it in the space so that the city and its inhabitants live their destiny—be it gentle or hard, heroic or nonheroic." This notion of destiny is critical to the Archupallas project and to the attitude and intention of the Open City in Ritoque. Destiny is not something to be imposed upon the city but allowed to unfold through time and space. It is, however, present within the city from its very beginning. Like a mirage, it is a mental image of city that is projected out of the physical and cultural context in which the city is sited. The theoretical foundation of the Archupallas project elaborates this through a discussion of Valparaíso as a city that has forgotten its destiny, lost its ability to see and construct its destiny, and is therefore a city of the blind. Valparaíso was positioned at the intersection of two axes that crossed in time: one, the

73.   Alberto Cruz in the Archupallas project, Fundamentos
de la Escuela de Arquitectura,
Universidad Católica de Valparaíso, 1971.

74.   "Una organización que
quiere un lugar para la vivienda
de sus organizados," Ibid.

north-south axis or route of passage connecting Panama to the Magallenes, and later New York to Antartica; and the east-west axis connecting Buenos Aires to the Pacific. Two axes: one, which is Chile—the length, and another running across through the Aconcagua River valley, following the snows to the sea. These axes intersect at the edge of the Pacific where Valparaíso was constructed. However, according to the Archupallas text, Valparaíso has lost the destiny of its location at the intersection of these two axes because it has lost the sea. Begun at the water's edge, attached to that edge because of a dependence on the sea as a transportation route, the city over time has begun to move up into the hills, "searching for the land . . . Valparaíso has forgotten its sea, lost its edge and border, the mystery of the union of the water with the earth, of water with the rock, with the mass of the land, of water and sand . . . (and) therefore, it has lost its form given by the sea." The city has grown outside of its destiny. This is open to interpretation, but the critical point is the notion of destiny as something that is, in a way, perceptible from a city's founding because it is absolutely linked to the physical and cultural context of that founding. And that the destiny of city, or *a* city, like a mirage, is a mental image connected to the possibility of an intact physical reality, and therefore the constructing of space and city merely pursues that mental image. But, precisely because that image is miragelike—illusive, not fixed—it operates as a proposition, a possibility on the structural level, not as a formula or prescriptive plan.

"The urbanist discovers the destiny of the city and *positions* it in the space so that the city and its inhabitants live their destiny—be it gentle or hard, heroic or nonheroic." If the destiny is a possibility, the key pragmatic questions are how is the destiny set in motion, how is it positioned in the space? The idea of destiny carries with it a premise of liberty. It is this liberty inside of the intention that gives spatial form to the destiny. Liberty to create that which life demands. Therefore, it is the intention that must be set in motion, established spatially, so that it structures the city's unfolding. This implies that order is built from the inside and not imposed from the outside. The project cites as a model the Gothic city and the Gothic cathedral, which, from the inside, organizes the city around it. As a seed of order, it forms the urban space and the city fabric. It informs the placement of functions and activities, and it establishes the spatial hierarchy radiating from it. It is absolutely attached to the structure of Gothic society, and therefore it initiates the city's destiny as it relates to its cultural site. By its siting, it initiates the city's destiny as it relates to its physical site.

coduños de Valparaiso
coduños de Valparaiso mirando el mar a través de los arboles.
lo que tanto se buscaba.
el mar a través de los arboles
la ola y la hoja

From the Archupallas project. "Destiny in the eye. The eye in the circulations."

The Archupallas project embraces both theoretically and practically this model of a seed of order that initiates city. The proposal again turns to Valparaíso to determine what it is that structures that city from the inside, what is the "sign of the city," and determines that it is the space of circulation: the streets and plazas. The streets because through them one engages the site, navigates the land—the ridges and valleys—moves across the land and through the city. The plazas because in them one engages others and public life, and because the plazas as the parochial centers link one engaged in public life to one's faith. It is not, however, the system of circulation itself but, more profoundly, the relationship of the space of circulation to the space of the individual as perceived through the eye. This is what makes it an interior proposition versus an exterior imposition. Implicit in its relationship to the eye of the individual is the sovereignty of the section—the rise and fall of the land. It is the extreme topography of the coastal site that invokes the destiny of Valparaíso and, in a related way, Archupallas. As the human gaze ascends it engages the trees, the sky. As it descends, it engages the earth and the sea.

"Destiny in the eye. The eye in the circulations. Circulations of destiny. Obtain the circulations—there is the battle." From this portion of the text, the proposition for Archupallas is invented. The actual site covers three hills of forested land overlooking the sea. Its destiny is initiated by the forming of three boulevards that navigate the ridges of the hills to connect the forested land to the sea and the sky through phenomena of perception. The boulevards are spatially formed by rows of trees whose trunks make a screen of right angles with the horizontal line between sea and sky. They establish a "measuring" and scaling of the space while they connect the space of the boulevard to the space of the sea through the relationship of the right angle. Each boulevard supports a plaza, the seed of the parish. One of the three boulevards attaches Archupallas to the amphitheater of Viña del Mar, making it the most significant of the three. As the generating element of the city, it becomes the focus of the proposition with the assumption that from its structure will grow the rest of the city thereby "positioning the destiny of the city in the space." The section of the land through which the boulevard passes is reconfigured to obtain a constant slope, augmenting the discovery of the sea through the trees and the focus of the space. The boulevard sponsors a series of interior streets and terraced mesas from which the neighborhoods will develop. The mesas are formalized balconies to the sea that then merge into the natural section of the hill. Ridge, boulevard, mesas, and freedom of

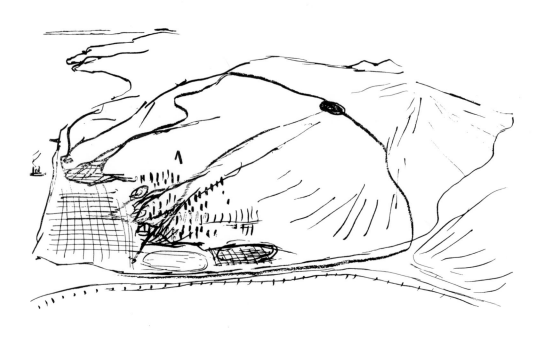

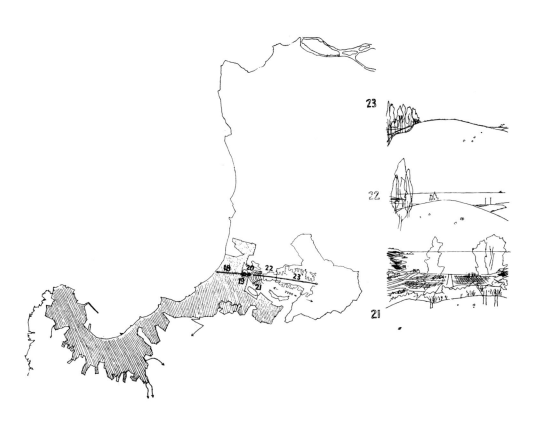

The Archupallas project in the hills east of Viña del Mar

development within this open structure are the four points of the proposition of Archupallas. The project proposes that the developers of Archupallas build the first three. "Of what does the rest of the urbanization consist given that it is only supported by these four points? It will be realized in correspondence with the ideas of the architect-urbanists as they will determine it. If the balconies (the mesas) produce buildings or not, if there will be school, commerce, etc., etc."

Archupallas is an important project to the discussion of the Open City in Ritoque for several reasons. As a predecessor to the Open City, it reveals an attitude about city making and urban settlement that affirms the notion of city as something that is structured from the inside to an extent, and in a manner, that allows for the open formation—the making physically manifest in form—of itself. At the same time it insists that this interior structure is the manifest making of a city's destiny that is an intact, however illusive, image of itself. The interior structure is the initiation of the city's destiny. In the project for Archupallas, the structuring device is physical—street, plaza, terraces—and even formal; it is a linear organization, a boulevard with trees. At Ritoque, the structuring device is a mental construction. But at both places, the structuring device is attached to a human phenomenological relationship to the land. One gets the impression that the Archupallas project was in a way an attempt to recuperate Valparaíso's lost destiny in which the mystery of the union of the sea to the earth, the land, the sky, and so on was to be acknowledged. However, the project remains only a suggestion because it was never realized, although it easily could have been as it respectfully addresses itself to certain pragmatic issues. The Open City, on the other hand, makes no pretense of pragmatism, and it continues to inspire its own continuity as a built reality that clearly positions itself within an image of a destiny remarkably similar to that interpreted as lost by Valparaíso. Parenthetically, Ritoque is located at the mouth of the Aconcagua River, which is considered to be the exact position of the east-west axis crossing Chile to connect Buenos Aires to the Pacific. It is through the Aconcagua River that the snows return to the sea. So Ritoque is more precisely located in the intersection of the two axes that cross Chile in time.

The Archupallas project brings into focus the concept of destiny and its attachment to the forming of city, which is an important concept to the Open City as well. Because the destiny is a mirage, an implication of the city formed, and because it is attached to the city from the very beginning, it is something that implies that the city is city from the moment of its founding and that its character is initiated at that moment. How long it takes to establish conventional urban density or build that character is an exterior issue. The importance of city founding and this idea of destiny is a significant component of the Latin American urban heritage. During the second stage of the colonization of the continent, city founding, which had been relatively ad hoc, was raised to a self-conscious and prestigious level. "The founding of a city was converted into a ritual which formalized the task of colonizing the new territories. The act of founding was accompanied by drawings or traces of the city and the assignment of territories to the colonists, remaining, literally and graphically, described in this document of vital political, administrative and urbanistic importance."[75] In the tradition of Spanish American cities, the Open City was founded as a city around specific foundational acts—it occurred in a similar self-conscious and ritualistic manner—and the poem *amereida* serves as the charter of that founding, the document or "trace" of the city. The intention of city appears in its name and its naming. The act of founding of the Spanish American cities conferred the status of city to even the most embryonic settlements. Alberto Cruz affirms that in the Spanish tradition the city was very much a place of contemplation first and that the status of city was conferred by the king for loyalty. In exchange for protection of the territory claimed for Spain and the extending of Spanish hospitality through land gifts that increased the size of the settlements, the king promised to sustain the city. The purpose of the city was very specifically settlement, at any cost, for Spain. At the Open City, the purpose is, metaphorically, settlement for poetry with loyalty toward America, and the concept of hospitality is a base for the communal activity.

The Renaissance architect Leon Battista Alberti claimed that the city has two meanings: a grouping of edifices in a certain pattern and a meeting of men. The Open City is composed of a grouping of edifices, although not in any discernible pattern. It was founded as a city, and there exists a precise intention to construct a communal field of activity based upon a certain way of acting. This field of activity is outlined in a charter, the *amereida,* and all issues important to it are debated in public forums. The physical environment of city is a consequence of this field of activity, not the reverse. The Open City stands in strong contrast to the hierarchical European Renaissance cities in which a built idealized architectural plan was expected to determine a higher state of living for all its citizens. Instead of an imposed geometrical order making neat packages into which the different types of citizens were

75. José Alcina Franch, in the exhibition catalogue La Cuidad Hispanoamericana, El Sueño de un Orden *(Centro de Estudios Históricos de Obras Públicas y Urbanismo, Ministerio de Obras Públicas y Urbanismo),* 120.

Along the approach to the palace, an agora was formed by a depression that was made in the grass plateau. Not unlike Mayan
ball courts in form and alignment, the depression aligns with the
cardinal points and is bounded on the western edge by a bosque
of trees. The bermed slope on the northern side of the agora is
most always in shadow, while the bermed slope on the southern
side is most always in light. The agora is ringed by sculptures, interrupting the surface of the land, which are the singular clues from
afar that this meeting place exists. From inside the agora, how-

ever, the space is clearly defined by the berm edges that mask off the more remote features of the landscape, producing a perceived lowering of the sky.

Throughout the site one finds numerous agora, large and small, accompanied by sculptures and poems built or inscribed into elements of the sites. The agoras are used in the Open City in their double sense, as both a place to meet and the act of meeting, and therefore they were some of the first elements to be laid onto the site and have a very important presence in the site. They are minimal in their construction, often only defined by paving, retaining walls, paths, sculptures, or built poems. As built outlines or marks of place within the continuity of the landscape, they both collect and disperse thought: thought collected through the meeting of the community and dispersed through individual contemplation.

placed in conjunction with a neat ordering of transportation, commerce, trade, religious activity, and education, the Open City mixes all. The dedication to a way of acting has no boundaries; it extends throughout the city and throughout the activities of the twenty-four-hour day.

For the builders of the Open City, the keys to urbanism are man—for it is man who is capable of poetic activity—and the collective energy of the community. It is not a theoretical urbanism, but one of action completely removed from the drawing board and transferred into the hands of the individuals working in community. It is an urbanism formed by the gestures and minds of the individuals and of the group. It is not surprising, then, that the first structures to be built were not churches or markets—power functions—but hospederías and agoras. "The lawful occupation of all societies that establish themselves, of all civilizations that appear. House man first, shelter him from storms and thieves, but above all arrange around him the peace of a hearth, do all that is necessary so that his existence unrolls its hours in harmony, without transgressing the laws of nature."[76] The house is the place that unfolds around the activities and gestures of the individual and in which one spends the most meaningful parts of the day. It is the place of renewal, and the hospedería, which is more than house, is, additionally, a place of meeting and exchange of individuals. It serves both the individual and the group whereas the agora is, specifically, the place that unfolds around the gestures of the community.

Traditionally, the Greek agora was constructed as a convener of the social group both functionally and urbanistically. It sustained an intense and varied concentration of activities that served daily life socially, commercially, and politically. Because of its role at the heart of daily life and because the members of the Open City are committed to the poetic manifestation of daily life, not the extraordinary event, the agora becomes an important component of the Open City. However, at the Open City, although the agora maintains its original purpose as a place of assembly, it does not serve to spatially or formally focus and organize the city. Instead, as places of contemplation, as well as of assembly, the agoras serve to focus mental as well as social activity. There is not one agora providing focus but numerous agoras dispersed in different settings throughout the natural site, interacting with different qualities of the site. These agoras are built spaces laid upon the sand as one would lay a picnic cloth down, or they are formed into the more solid ground by depression. Like the Greek agoras they are built spaces, not the space resulting from the construction of buildings belonging to other

76.   "Occupation licite de toute société qui s'installe, de toute civilisation qui apparaît. Loger les hommes d'abord, les mettre à l'abri des intempéries et des voleurs, mais surtout aménager autour d'eux la paix d'un foyer, faire tout ce qu'il faut pour que l'existence déroule ses heures dans l'harmonie, sans transgression dangereuse des lois de nature." Le Corbusier, entretien avec les étudiants.

agendas. They are a deliberate building of space that hosts the coming together of people in urban activity, hosts the interaction and the social
contract of the polis. Yet in addition to serving group contemplation, they
also serve to assist individual contemplation, and, in this, they contain the tension between community and individual that is historically one of the most
challenging points related to urbanism.

The agora is clearly an essential component of the city as defined by a
communal field of activity because it initiates that field of activity. City, by
this definition, implies the ability and ambition of all citizens to participate in
urban life in a direct and unmediated way. This of course has implications on
the size of the city. Aristotle argued that "to decide questions of justice and
in order to distribute the offices according to merit it is necessary for the citizens to know each other's personal characters" and therefore the size of the
polis must be more than ten but less than ten thousand. The advent of the industrial era and the construction of megalopolises that inconceivably exceed
even the ideal modern city of 3 million inhabitants[77] have clearly obliterated
the possibility of unmediated participation in all, or even most, aspects of the
social, commercial, and political fields of activity of city by all citizens. It
seems that a key question becomes whether or not it is size that determines
city, or does a city determine its own size. Similarly, is the status of megalopo-
lis a prerequisite to modern city, and especially to modern city in a South
American context where industry is less ubiquitous and usually highly con-
centrated? Is industry an absolutely necessary prerequisite to modernity,
meaning that anything less is merely a town or village? The Open City has
a rather insignificant population—around a hundred in the community at
most, not all of whom are permanent residents—but it does not have the
rural structure or quality of a town or village. Nor does it have the agrarian
impetus of town or village; it is neither agrarian nor industrial. It does not
have the land-as-commodity mentality of suburban construction. And of significance is the fact that visitors to the city almost unanimously approach it as
an urban construction even though it is built in the sand, over the dunes.

But beyond size, the Open City provokes the critical question of
whether one can discuss city, or even urban settlement, as something that is
related to communal participation in a modern context, or is it—as it relates
to Greek precedent of urban culture—an anachronism after the industrial
revolution?[78] Perhaps it is, or perhaps it attaches itself to issues of modern
urbanism through another door, through its *process* and *intention*.

77.   *Le Corbusier's utopian
proposal for the city of 3 million
inhabitants.*

78.   *A bias toward Greek
precedent and thought is not
isolated to the adoption of the
agora as an urban model alone.
Throughout the work of the*
*Catholic University of Valpa-
raíso one finds reverberations of
this bias: the amereida as a
foundation myth analogous to
the Aeneid, references to
Greek mythology, love of the
mythological as one form of
poetry, and so forth.*

Prior to the Industrial Revolution, the urban construction may have been what French architectural historian Françoise Choay calls, "a semiotic system whose elements were related synchronically within the context of rules and a code practiced by inhabitant and planner alike. By virtue of its relationship with all the other social systems (political power, learning, economy, religion), the urban system asserted itself as one of communication and information."[79] In other words, the inhabitants of the city were integrated into the physical and social structure of the city through the semiotic system and, therefore, engaged in an unmediated relationship with their physical and cultural context. Their position and meaning within the city were integrally related to the physical space of the city, and the physical structure communicated to them their roles within that structure. The medieval city, which the theoretical portion of the Archupallas project cites, is one of the clearer examples of this preindustrial semiotic urban structure.

The Industrial Revolution, however, initiated a radical transformation of the spatial organization of the city as rural immigrants flooded the city in ignorance of the functioning and significance of the urban structure. An impoverishment of the previous semantic system occurred as the city's growing urban organization was determined solely by the capitalist-industrialist ambition. The power of the economic drive replaced the complex preindustrial structure in which were integrally bound all systems of urban life: social, political, religious, and economic. The city lost its richness, it became monosemantic. The inhabitants of the city are subjected to a spatial order emptied of its traditional meaning and one with which they no longer share an intimate or immediate relationship. They are no longer involved in the shaping and forming of their city, and, very importantly, with the advent of technologically mediated systems of communication, they even lose direct knowledge of their city and its events, which become increasingly more abstract. Telegraph and newspapers replace oral communication, and the railroad displaces the boundaries of the space.

The radical transformation of the spatial order of the city obviously provoked a transformation of the mentality of the city dweller. "Following the loss of partial conscious control and of implicit subconscious control, those actually experiencing the urban phenomenon came to consider it as something alien. They no longer felt inside the process and determined by it; they remained outside, observing the transformation with the eye of the spectator. The inhabitant suddenly saw the city as transformed by that 'incidence of strangeness,' which Claude Lévi-Strauss considers the prerequisite of eth-

79.   *Françoise Choay,* The
Modern City: Planning in the
19th Century (New York:
George Braziller, 1969), 7.

nological observation. Furthermore the attitude that the city is something subject to examination has been made possible by a simultaneous evolution in the structure of knowledge." Objectivity provided by historical perspective creates a reviewing of society's material and spiritual productions and a transformation in the mental processes and in the conceptual tools of those involved with the making and inhabiting of the city. Analysis and critique sponsors a new type of self-conscious planning and even planning as a profession. "The process of urban organization at this point loses its original immediacy, as it now evolves about an object that has been removed from its context by analysis: for the first time the umbilical cord has been cut, so to speak, and the city subjected to critical examination. Consequently, the planning which was to emerge specifically from this critical approach may be termed *critical planning*." [80]

If one accepts that the modern city is both a result of the technological developments of the industrial era that created a powerful economic impetus for change and an application of a self-conscious and critical process of planning for that change—again, modernity related to the pragmatics of technology and the theoretics of critique—it seems that the Open City, while not in any manner resembling the modern western metropolis of today, or even more specifically the few modern Latin American metropolises, does engage and involve itself with modern urban culture through the processes of thinking and conceptualizing about modern urban culture and spatial structure. It specifically employs modern theoretical and conceptual tools: analysis and critique filtered by phenomenology, as is exemplified in the theoretical premise and urban proposition of the Archupallas project, as well as the application of modern poetic methodologies to initiate the criticism and proposition of architectural and urban space. These tools and methodologies belong implicitly and explicitly to an ideology that is not only the *foundation* for the production of physical space but also the *way* to producing physical space. The significance of the result is, therefore, that the Open City refers explicitly and implicitly to this ideology. In doing so it recuperates semantic richness and the individual is integrally included in the semiotic system.

The critical planning tools of modern urbanism were mostly applied to the reorganization and rehabilitation of existing city structures that industrial growth had placed in a certain state of physical crisis. At the Open City, the analogous tools are applied to a virgin condition of urban settlement and to a

80.   Ibid., 9–10.

virgin site. There are modern precedents for this in the models of the Utopian Socialists that approximate this condition and, therefore, have a similar scale. The phalanstère of Fourier, which was later built by the industrialist Godin in Guise, France, as well as Robert Owen's squares and New Harmony, Indiana, were also generated by an application of critical methodologies not to existing urban disorder but to new propositions of urban settlement. Within these imaginary cities and the built experiments they induced, the condition of alienation that resulted from the collision between the monosemantic industrial ambition and the traditional city was theoretically annulled by a positivist belief that industrial society was actually a promise of liberation through the machine that would transform modern men and women and their world. Whereas traditional hierarchical systems of power were confining, the machine was to liberate the individual to his or her own devices within the equality of labor. All this, provided that cities would be designed to create a harmonious structure in which the machine and labor were integrated into the systematization of city. These cities used simple geometric ordering devices—geometry represented truth as well as beauty—and they adopted a concept of space that was dependent upon the breaking apart of the mass of the city to allow air, light, and greenery to permeate the space of the city. Air, light, and greenery, essential elements for physical hygiene, were symbolic of progress.

The significance of these models is that they, like the Open City, strive to recover semantic richness. They do not see industrialization and economic efficiency as the sole driving principle of urban planning but, instead, out of a critical conceptualization of the relationship of society and machine, they form an ideology and a model for implementing that ideology. The model creates and orders the conditions for communal participation in which hierarchical structure is eradicated. However, in these models the communal participation is prescribed by the physical model and by the industrialist father figure who creates or even builds, in the case of Godin, the model. At the Open City, the relationship is reversed: the communal field of activity, the "meeting of men," creates the physical city. The physical city and meeting of men are integrally attached. And while the utopian models remain fixed in their size, form, and organization, the Open City is open. Its physical size, form, and organization change. New buildings are added, some are added on to, some parts are removed, new activities are accommodated, changing the focus and form of the city, and the process continues. Additionally, the models of the Utopian Socialists regard nature and physical site as a hygienic commodity. It is pulled into the model but not integrated into the semiotic system. Whereas at the Open City the physical site, which extends beyond the immediate into the context of the whole continent, is absolutely a semantic component of the semiotic system. Because of their size and distribution of density, the models of Fourier and Owens do not achieve urban character. For the same reasons, neither does the Open City. However, in these models, size is defined by the model, whereas at the Open City, size and density are not prescribed. Theoretically, the city could grow to achieve what one might consider to be urban density, but, in truth, this is not really an issue. What exists is a result of what has been achieved within an intention of city. What will exist in the future will be a result of the same.

Another point of comparison between the above-mentioned urban models and the Open City, perhaps the more significant comparison, is between the bearings of their ideologies. Both attempt to recover semantic richness—meaning—through a critical approach to the modern city that, through ideation, prompts a proposition about urban settlement. However, the modern utopian models as products of the Enlightenment refer to an ideology fueled by the insistence that reason is the supreme value in the world as it relates to, and is employed by, man: through reason one can understand social activity, behavior, and structure, since it is assumed that all men are alike, and understanding social activity, reason can operate on it, organize it, and build space that accommodates and/or transforms it. The exclusive faith in reason is the limitation of these models. The ideology of the Open City, on the other hand, displaces reason for poetry. Truth is related not to the rational but to the mysterious. Not to the organizing of reality but to its discovery and transformation. And poetry, not as the gratuitous overlay of sentiment to augment the world organized by reason but, rather, as a specific mental field with a potency that supersedes reason in that it does not confine itself to only the obvious and logical but, more important, admits the illogical and illusive of reality into its field of activity. Poetry as a faculty of perception and proposition. "The society prophesied by the poet's word cannot be confused with political utopia. Reason creates darker jails than theology. Man's enemy is named Urizen (Reason), the 'god of systems', the prisoner of himself. Truth does not proceed from reason, but from poetic perception, that is, from imagination."[81] The socialization of this imagination at Ritoque creates a communal field of activity that more closely resembles the communities dreamed and promoted by the poets William Blake or Novalis: communities dedicated to the collective production of poetry in which man

81.   *Blake as paraphrased by Paz in* The Bow and the Lyre, *218–219.*

Casa de los Nombres

is inserted into history through his relationship to the poetic word, which comes from within rather than through his relationship to systems of power—state, church, industry; the throne, altar and machine—which impose truths from without.

9   *O le pauvre amoureux des pays chimériques!*
Faut-il le mettre aux fers, le jeter à la mer,
Ce matelot ivrogne, inventeur d'Amériques
Dont le mirage rend le gouffre plus amer?[82]

Although it distances itself from the didactic utopian visions, whether modern or classical, one cannot deny that the Open City, its philosophical base and way of acting, has a certain utopian propensity. In its repudiation of contemporary values associated with the production of architecture and its "leap into a new state of being in which (these) contemporary values are totally transformed or turned upside down," it implies a utopian drive.[83] Disharmony within the relationships of the built environment to the natural environment and to the basic existential state of humanity is to be transformed by a shift of focus from the product, which creates this disharmony, to the process, which engages reality through the poetic state of man. The poetic condition attempts to reconfigure the relationship—the space—between ourselves and reality by removing the mediation, the distancing, set up by the drive toward product, toward activity as commodity and, therefore, life as commodity. Despite this propensity, however, the Open City is not a *model* for social, or even architectural, reform because it generates more problems than solutions. It is more a laboratory and does not pretend that its discoveries are applicable outside of itself.

That the Open City functions more like a laboratory than a model of the poetic intention is critical to the resulting work and the work's communication of this poetic intention. Its functioning as a laboratory is dependent on the purity of the process. For this reason, all the work is supported by funds internal to the city and school, and time constraints are of absolutely no importance.

More important, with regard to the laboratory, it is not the proof that is important—because art does not advance as science does by proofs and errors—but the process of discovery. This process is not fueled by reason but ignited by poetic impulse that connects the field of inquiry to an inner level of consciousness in which the poetic mind resides. In this sense, the utopian

82.   *O the poor lover of imaginary countries!*
Should we put him in irons or throw him to the sea,
This drunken sailor, inventor of Americas
Of which the mirage makes the abyss more bitter?

Charles Baudelaire, "Le Voyage," as found in The Flowers of Evil & Paris Spleen (Brockport, NY: BOA Editions, Ltd., 1991), 254.

83.   Frank E. Manuel and Fritzie P. Manuel, Utopian Thought in the Western World (Cambridge, Mass.: Harvard University Press, 1980), 8. A precise definition of utopian thought is illusive as "in the course of time, 'proper' utopias, discussions of utopian thought, and portrayals of utopian states of consciousness have so interpenetrated that the perimeters of the concept of utopia have to be left hazy" (p. 5). But a consensus of opinion assumes an emotional attitude in which the utopian proposition is a reaction to and proposed cure for a state of unhappiness or discord (the anti-utopia) within at least one area—the critical one for the utopian. Through utopia, it is to be supposed, if it is not directly stated, that future happiness and harmony are secured.

Casa de los Nombres.

propensity of the Open City is much closer to the "eupsychia" fabricated by Rousseau, an "optimum state of consciousness, in a society whose material structures tend to fade into the background."[84] Rousseau's eupsychia, however, is not an urban utopia although it confronts the two most challenging questions, historically, related to urbanism—the balancing of societal cohesion with individual expression and the form of the social group that will provide this balance—and he grapples with the institutional arrangements for achieving and perpetuating the eupsychia. The Open City, as a laboratory, is essentially this same type of institution developed by the Catholic University of Valparaíso although the intent is very specifically focused toward a poetic eupsychia.

The focus of the Open City is poetic with an assumption that poetry applies not merely to the creative production of art but also to the way in which one lives one's life, both individually and in community. But it is not a totalitarian proposition; most utopias, including the eupsychia of Rousseau, propose solutions encompassing all aspects of utopian life: social, moral, political, religious, and intellectual. It is evident, though, that the intent to poetically fuse art and life has ultimately created a reform or, at least, translation of many aspects of the community life.

Although the utopian propensity exists at the Open City, there are three key issues that separate it from utopian status. The first is the issue of immutability. Utopia projects a model for an ideal society that is itself ahistorical and acultural, transcending particularities and peculiarities of any given period. It is a changeless society with immutable institutions. Whether it be achieved in stone, as Alberti aspired to, or through a system of laws, or through a moral systematic education, the goal was something so perfect it would never need to be changed. This is hardly the goal or reality at the Open City. If anything, mutability is one of the few laws in Ritoque. Each project is loyal to the muse of reinvention, and no work is ever considered complete and finished, or sacred to the exclusion of transformation.

Second is the issue of generality and universality. "The ideal condition should have some measure of generality, or it becomes merely a narcissistic yearning."[85] The work of the Open City does not propose an application of its specific combination of working and living on any level of universality. It does not even suggest its own continuity. In fact, in many cases the sons and daughters of the founders have grown up living in the city to become architects who do not work in the city. Because it is founded around an attitude and not a model, and because the attitude can be un-

84.   Ibid., 439.

85.   Ibid., 7.

earthed but not taught, it is a somewhat fragile proposition. One could argue that the attitude, and even methodologies, might sustain a certain universal application, and it is this that prevents it from sinking into narcissistic yearning. The attitude is certainly capable of inspiring a way of working that would create extremely diverse and distinct results in different physical and cultural contexts. Precisely because it is an attitude dependent on a certain theoretical premise that is absolutely attached to both physical and cultural context, any dissemination, however, would inadvertently produce significant translation of the theoretical underpinnings and also of its metaphysical properties and biases. Any universality would exist as an enigmatic proposition rather than as a fixed set of approaches or procedures.

Third, the concept of utopia is born out of two very ancient beliefs that have molded and nurtured it: the Judeo-Christian belief in a paradise that was created with the world in the form of the Garden of Eden, which endures although mankind is no longer part of it, and the Hellenic myth of an ideal city built by men for men without the approval or aid of the gods. Nostalgia for a return or reappropriation of this heaven on earth is one of the key corollaries to utopian thought. It is not an accident that utopia was often equated with the New World of the Americas or that the first true utopian model appeared in 1516, twenty-four years after the discovery of the Americas. Thomas More's Utopia, the country of "nowhere," was "discovered" by a Portuguese mariner who had supposedly been a member of Amerigo Vespucci's expeditions. Vespucci himself wrote in his *Novus Mundus* of 1503 "the people live in agreement with nature. They have no property; instead, all things are held in community. They live without king and without any form of authority, and each one is his own master." The Americas were expected, by Europeans, to be the home of Rousseau's noble savage, the place where the natural state of man still existed in an ideal relationship with nature. Nostalgia for this natural state is at the foundation of utopian models with the implication that if one attains what one had before, life will become simpler and the injustice invented by man will evaporate: the Golden Age will be restored. The attitude and work of the Open City rejects completely the nostalgic mode that is an auxiliary of utopia. In the poem *amereida,* it is nostalgia, and particularly this European nostalgia, that has extinguished the songs received from within the American continent and erased the historical force nurtured there. In other words, it is the nostalgic drive of Europe that is significantly responsible for the conquering, enslavement, and destruction of the same Native American populations that it intellectually ennobled.

At the same time, it is nostalgia for the native condition that also obscures the reality of this condition that is a meeting of races, and it denies this reality its future. The temptation of nostalgia is "an odor of promises, of easy futures which corrode energy—those windows of hope which speak up for the night and make our images to disappear."[86]

Instead of a nostalgic relationship to its physical and historical context, the work at the Open City deals with its context as an essential reality. It is not abstract or intellectual, both prerequisites of nostalgia.

Tangentially, a comparison can be made here to Paolo Soleri's project in the Arizona desert, Arcosanti. Although the project exhibits a similar drive to reattach man to nature, Arcosanti is so completely embedded in a nostalgia for the ideal ecological state of man in relationship to nature, and in utopia making, that it reduces the nature it is in search of reattachment with to a commodity. Arcosanti does propose a totalitarian and immutable model for ecological utopia. This model requires a significant urban density and systematized social order that accommodates work—architectural, agricultural, artisanal, and ecological—alongside education and enjoyment of free time. The physical reality of this nostalgia for the ideal ecological state finds its inspiration in forms that mimic the cave pueblos of the Native Americans of the southwestern United States but not in the tribal structure. It is an architecture that is, today, being built as it was designed in 1970, the year the Open City was inaugurated. The difference between the two works lies in the attitude with regard to nature—whether it is a gift or a commodity—and whether man's creative activity is in service of an ecological use of the commodity or in service of poetic activity that attempts to join the essential qualities of man to the essential qualities of nature, to join the gift and the one who accepts the gift. One proposes a utopian model while the other suggests a way toward discovery.

Utopia, as well as a set of conditions, is a philosophical stance. U-topia—no place—implies a state of existence so perfect that it cannot exist in an imperfect mundane world. It is by nature a goal, a philosophic model that mundane reality attempts to mimic. It is no-place, in reality, which as a model, however, is capable of creating place within reality. In their essay "La Cuidad Abierta: De la Utopía al Espejismo," Alberto Cruz and Godofredo Iommi maintain that the Open City, instead of being utopia—no-place, no-*lugar*—is *sin-lugar*, without place, meaning: a place that does exist within the reality of the mundane but has the quality of being different or less than

86. *"un olor de promesas / de hábiles futuros que corroen la energía—esas ventanas de las esperanzas que chistan por las noches y desvanecen nuestras figuras,"* Iommi, amereida, 11.

Beyond the Music Room, a bamboo road heads off into the high
sand dunes to end at the top of a large dune that commands a
view of the entire coastal plane and Pacific below and which beck-
ons to the upper plateau across the highway. This is the site of the
Casa de los Nombres (the House of Names), which is the only
building, to date, built in the raw sand completely open to the
forces of the winds, the consequent movement of the sands, the
unshaded passage of the sun, and the clarity of the night sky. It is
a room built under the surface of the dune to accommodate four

what we expect of reality in the physical world. In other words, it is a place with a mundane physical existence whose defining characteristic is to not have the density (*espesor*) of the real world—like a mirage (*espejismo*). A mirage does not have density. It is nothing more than pure appearance or apparition. It is a real presence with a less than real dimension, like the mirage in the desert that makes the oasis visible. The oasis does exist somewhere else in the desert. It is not invented. It is a reality although it is in another place. Through the oblique reflection of the phenomena of mirage its idea, its image, its presence is accessible. The mirage marks this *other place* in the space.

The less than real dimension of the mirage that is reduced is the temporal dimension, time. The mirage contains neither "was" nor "will be" within its presence as these are not required in the mere presentation. From this position, Iommi and Cruz then ask the theoretical question as to whether one can construct a mirage and what it means to construct with a less than real temporal dimension—to construct space that does not have density in time and, therefore, is pure appearance or apparition. The implication is that the Open City attempts to address these questions in its work and that perhaps it is an attempt to construct a mirage. There are two critical conditions for the attempt, both of which imply a reversal of the traditional orientation of process to product. To construct the mirage, the construction must not be founded in the expectation or fixed, in a prescribed manner, in a future, in a predetermined image that it is constantly attempting to catch up with. It also requires the modification of the relationship with what is implied by permanence. The task does not have to have a future. As a mirage, its "was" and "will be" is irrelevant.

The Open City then, as an attempt to construct the mirage, is not Utopia, but city in a pure form as Iommi and Cruz contend:

•

A work for the pure apparition—is it not truly "poiesis"? [87] If opened up in the apparition is all of its manifestations, its being, mere apparitions, appearances, mirages.

Perhaps poetry, in fact, reduces this dimension to which we are alluding (time); perhaps it assumes the suspension of all disbelief, as Coleridge claimed, and expresses itself from its belief in all work. From this being possible, the possibility of a concrete and real task unfolds, of a complex of poetic works whose manifestation is only to appear. Would not this complex of works be "city"? [88]

•

87.   Poeisis: (from the Greek poiesis: *creation, making, poem*) the action or faculty of producing or doing something especially creatively. Webster's Third New International Dictionary.

88.   "Un trabajo para la pura aparición ¿no es realmente "poiesis"? Si así fuera se abren en ella todas sus manifestaciones, su ser, meras apariciones, apariencias, espejismos. Tal vez la poesía, de hecho, resta esa dimensión a que aludimos; tal vez supone la suspensión de toda incredulidad, según Coleridge, y se expresa desde esa creencia a todos los oficios. De ser esto posible se abre la posibilidad de un quehacer concreto y real, de un complejo de oficios poéticos cuyo manifestación es sólo aparecer. ¿No será ese complejo de oficios "cuidad"? "la cuidad abierta: de la utopía al espejismo," Revista Universitaria No. 9 (Publicacion de la Pontificía Universidad Católica de Chile).

hundred people as a meeting and exhibition space. Discussed, elaborated, and logistically planned over two years, it was built in eight weeks during which four hundred people worked continuously. To create the room, its area was first mapped onto the surface of the dune not by posts and cord but by the placement of bodies within the site: twenty-nine people, twenty-nine names. Then a grid of twenty-nine concrete pillars, twenty-six feet high, were driven into the sand at each location until their tops were level with the convex surface of the dune. The sand was excavated to create a concave bowl for the volume of the room. One pillar had to be removed to allow a small backhoe room in which to maneuver. The pillar was never replaced, and its absence remains in the space. Once the room was hollowed out and the pillars were stabilized, wood and cable trussed members were set into place, and a covering of industrial fiberglass cloth was laid over the structure. The room below the covering is spacious and light filled, opening up to the leeward side.

The idea of a group of works oriented only toward their own apparition—in other words, oriented toward their own processes of becoming—as forming city relies on the correspondence between "poiesis" and "city." *Poiesis,* meaning the "action or faculty of producing or doing something especially creatively," denotes the act of creativity, not the result. Yet poiesis, from the Greek, also means poem, the result. So bound up within the word is the process and the product and the implication that the product, the poem, is merely the manifestation of the process, not the process enslaved to the product. Also, poiesis, the creative act, requires the suspension of disbelief. It is disbelief that paralyzes the creative process. One must believe and desire to create. Therefore, in its capacity to believe, poiesis creates from out of the void, it creates something from out of nothing; and, believing in all things, it is capable of being the initiator of all tasks that form the communal field of city, whether those tasks are inherently poetic (religious functions) or conventionally mundane (communal functions). Together, these two sides of the word "poesis" relate to the concept of city through the concept of founding as the initiator of a city's destiny: that city is not oriented toward the production of organized structures and buildings nor is it what it physically becomes through arbitrary needs and haphazard solutions but, more important, that it is what it is intended to be at the moment of its conception, at the moment when one suspends disbelief and its destiny appears through poiesis, at that time in which "was" or "will be" is irrelevant. The physical city then is the marking of its destiny in the space, the engaging of the mirage in physical dialogue.

At the Open City, the concept of city as a complex of poetic works whose manifestation is only pure apparition has created a group of works that derive their material form from their own process of coming to be. The works, the buildings and agoras, reveal their processes of ideation and of physical making. Both the physical making and the ideation are integral parts of the semiotic structure of the projects and of the city. Therefore, they are apparent in the physical results. Additionally, the projects, through their semantic engagement of the landscape and the space of Ritoque, serve as apparitions that reveal the presence of the space.

Implicit within the idea of city as mirage are two concepts that form a distinct connection to the philosophical world of modern poetry: one is a spatial conception and the other a temporal conception. The spatial conception implicit within mirage is in the fact that the phenomenon of mirage is produced only through reflection. Mirages are illusive. When fixed on, they disappear. They can only be seen from an oblique position in space. Modern

While the pillars physically map the surface of the dune as it was at the moment of its excavation—for the dunes are always moving—the roof recreates, represents, rephrases the dune's formal and physical phenomena. The original surface of the dune, formed by the activity of the wind on the sand, is translated into a covering, not roof, which is light, airy, and translucent. With the wind, the sand moves over the surface of the new "dune" and recedes, and voices seem to emanate from the earth itself. Elsewhere on the site, from above and below, the construction ap-

pears as nomadic tent, sail, fallen glider. At the same time it presents itself as an amplified segment of the continuous structure and profile of the dunes, revealing the essential qualities of the sands through immediate quotation. As the fluid and primordial state of the land, of the mountains that can be seen in the distance, the dunes are always moving and reforming. The Casa de los Nombres, as built, is a meditation on this as it oscillates between its reference to the mountains or the dunes and to the precise moment in time it physically captures within the contin-

uum of the dunes' movement and transformation. Simultaneously, it is about light, opaque or translucent, about reflection and refraction, about the rainwater that is channelled along the truss lines, about the sand, its warmth and light, about the wind and its voice, about congregation and its voices, about the nomadic movement of people across the dunes, about being under the dune, about the night sky from a privileged position on the beach. And, inadvertently, about the unpredictability of the winds that do what you least expect, when you least expect it: the room was oriented ac-cording to the prominent direction of the coastal winds so that the entry would remain clear and protected from the sand's migration. After being built, however, it was discovered that the winds are not always as they seem, and therefore the sand, with a mind of its own, enters the room in peculiar places.

poetry and modern art understood well that reality was not to found within direct observation or narration of life but in the correspondences between phenomena, between signs, concepts, and mental images. They understood that appearances are relative and arbitrary, merely masks for the fluid apparitions of true presence, which cannot be called up on command. These apparitions must be teased out through poetic engagement of language and, oftentimes, through radical methodologies that force language to unmask itself. The apparitions appear at the periphery of vision, through the oblique, when you are no longer fixing your gaze through the field of reason toward goals and purposes. Words and language, removed from direct conversation to an oblique position through poetry, discover the apparitions. The concept of mirage implies its own revelation, meaning that in the believing that it is there—through the suspension of disbelief—presence appears in the form of image.

The temporal conception implicit within mirage is absolutely related to the idea that time as a pure presence has no density or thickness. Modernism in poetry, as a belief and search for pure presence, unshackled itself from the past. It maintained a naive faith in the future that was manifested in the present as the implication of, and direct connection to, the future. The present is the phenomenon of time passing and moving toward the future. It is time in real form: time experienced, not abstracted. Immediate and pure. Modernism was an attempt to locate itself in the present, in a pure way, to uncover and attach to a concept of time as pure presence, pure experience, something outside of history and its filtering process. For this, again, the concept of "was" and "will be" is irrelevant. Since city as mirage negates the historical concept of time that is a prerequisite for nostalgia, as a corollary it rejects the concept of utopia as a nostalgic desire to return to a more perfect era or as a futuristic model to be pursued.

City as mirage, as pure apparition, as related to its founding and, by extension, its destiny—again, one returns, inevitably, to the concept of city related specifically to the Latin American context. In essence, the Open City is a city in the Latin American vein but operated on with the conceptual and critical methodologies supplied by modernism and specifically by modern poetry. With regard to the concept of city initiated by its founding, the concept of the physical city being an unfolding of the destiny opened in the founding, and the establishment of a pact of communal participation of settlement, the Open City is a critical transformation of the embryonic Latin American urban settlements. But whereas in the traditional Latin American city one finds that meaning is dependent upon the formal structure—the plaza mayor,

the grid and block system—and its symbolic function as a model for colonialization, at the Open City one discovers meaning that is relatively raw, unmediated and transparent. The city is nothing more than its semantic structure, its meaning, and this semantic structure is fluid and light instead of fixed and authoritarian.

Where the Open City differs most from the traditional model is in its conscious rejection of urbanism as related to imposed formal ordering devices, in its rejection of the inheritance of the model. It is here that the critical transformation takes on most significance because the discarding of the didactic model means a complete transformation of the city's relationship to the landscape and the possibility of a recuperation of the solidarity between man and nature that was the foundation of the pre-Hispanic cultures. The systematic deployment of the traditional Latin American urban model as a carpet draped over the landscape, walled for defense, meant a distinct segregation of city/settlement and nature. Sited for reasons of trade, defense, the promise of natural treasure, hygienic convenience, and water supply, the model negotiated the landscape as best it could, sometimes in contention with the topography or previous indigenous settlement. This model—its existence, form, and strategic deployment—stands in contrast to the pre-Hispanic indigenous settlement in which nature occupied a sacred and elite position completely integrated into the form, functioning, and existential meaning of settlement. The traditional Latin American city is just that: traditional. Its meaning is in its connection to tradition, to history and its role in history, as was provided by its Spanish lineage. The didactic model supplied the unmistakable trace of lineage to which nature was subjected. The Open City on the other hand is not about a connection through physical trace but about the discovery of presence in nature. It is a critical rejection of the model to commit to a recognition of the American continent as a gift.

 su tierra así transida

> *¿no expondrá en la carne*

un ritmo

> *que mueva a lenguaje*

>> *porque sin lenguaje*

todas las rutas hacia nuestra intimidad

>> *aunque se adueñen*

deforman y engañan[89]

89. "the earth so overcome / is there not exposed in the flesh // a rhythm / which moves to language / because without language // all roads to our intimacy / even as they are possessed // deform and deceive," Iommi, amereida, 45.

That the discovery is through poetic means, not maps and compasses, and that it is focused upon the metaphysical relationship of man with his earth, not merely on territorial quantification, is because of this characterization of the earth as a gift. It is a gift with sacred properties of magic and mystery. Recognition that the earth is holy is probably one of the oldest certitudes of the Native American world and Latin America, as the meeting between this certitude and the Catholicism of Latin culture has conceived a sensuous and extremely tactile culture.[90] This heritage of tactility, versus abstraction, is very much infused into the pedagogic and experiential focus of the work of the Catholic University of Valparaíso, which sincerely attempts to recuperate a more immediate and intimate relationship between the members of the school and the natural world.

In the Native American religions, man's role with regard to the natural world is as guardians: one can not own what belongs to the gods. At the Open City this attitude prevails. Acceptance of the gift implies an acknowledgment of its sacredness and the assumption of responsibility for its guardianship by all. Because it is not about land as commodity, it is not about ownership. Therefore, the land is held in common. There are no individual sites or boundaries. There are no fences delineating separation of territory from the continuity of the land, the water, the sky, the winds. And all are responsible for its caretaking, which includes, most significantly, the *responsibility* of discovery. Language occupied in poetic activity and the concept of travesía secure this discovery and the acknowledgment of the gift, its acceptance. The acceptance constitutes the beginning of the recuperation of the more intimate relationship between the members of the school and the natural world that was inherent in the native religions. Yet, they approach this relationship through modern mental processes.

Within the native religions of the Americas, nature's structure is analogous to sacred structure, to the structure of the world of the gods: their comings and goings, their wants and desires, their anger and contentment. And being analogous and visible, nature's structure provides access to the gods. It is through nature that direct and unmediated communication with the gods occurs. Natural phenomena that are interpreted as representations of the personalities and traits of the gods are considered physical manifestations of the gods while other natural phenomena are the actual presence of the god. Space and time are integrally attached to each other through the personification of the gods in natural phenomena. The sun, the planet Venus, constellations, other celestial objects—as the presence of the gods—move

90. *Fuentes,* The Buried
Mirror, *347.*

through the space of the sky and the landscape, marking out the cycles and rhythms of time that rotate and circle in place. Their time and space forms man's time and space, his societal structure and, consequently, his constructions. Whether one refers to Mayan ceremonial centers that embedded the Mayan calendar—a complex interlocking of the cycles of the sun, the moon and Venus—into their urban spaces through the formation of precise networks of axial alignments attached to celestial appearances, disappearances, and confluences, or to the Aztec cities that built physical markers and doorways through which the sun or moon could enter or leave the space, or to the Incan marking of the landscape, on a colossal scale, with built lines that orientated the Incans to their calendar as delineated by the movement and timing of the constellations—a physical time map in the landscape,[91] or to the pueblos of the North American Southwest, the integration of time and space *through* natural phenomena, through nature as it is experienced by man, is a distinguishing character of the pre-Hispanic American cultures. And because the analogical system is both set up and interpreted by man, and it directly constructs space for the gods in which men operate as well, man is absolutely included in the relationship.

Man is integrally attached to the natural world in the pre-Hispanic culture through the semiotic structure of the culture, its space and its cities. This structure is ordered by nature because it is through nature that power is assembled and distributed. Political power is derived from religious power, and religious power is held by those who have direct communication with the gods, those who read the sky and the signs of the earth, those who are the guardians of time. The sky is the organizer of the semiotic structure that orders all aspects of the society and its space: "the cult of the gods, the wisdom of the destinies, the basic duties of man in his belonging to his family, group, town, chiefdom, his activities as a farmer, warrior, artist, merchant or in any other profession. In brief, to exist for the MesoAmericans one had to observe the sky. Without the skywatchers the ethos of this people, its distinguishing spirit, its own genius would not have developed."[92]

Within the work of the Catholic University of Valparaíso man is also attached to nature, integrally attached to nature, through semiotic structure. However, nature is not the organizer of the structure but is one element within it. Poetry is another element. Moreover poetry and language engaged in poetic activity occupy a more elite position because they serve as the initiator—*initiator*, not organizer. Poetry returns the mesoamerican sky in that it reveals the sky as a dominant field of the natural site. Yet poetry also replaces

91. "In that Empire, the craft of Cartography attained such Perfection that the Map of a Single province covered the space of an entire City, and the Map of the Empire itself an entire Province. In the course of Time, these Extensive maps were found somehow wanting, and so the College of Cartographers evolved a Map of the Empire that was of the same Scale as the Empire and that coincided with it point for point. Less attentive to the study of Cartography, succeeding Generations came to judge a map of such Magnitude cumbersome, and, not without Irreverence, they abandoned it to the Rigors of sun and Rain. In the western Deserts, tattered Fragments of the Map are still to be found, sheltering an occasional Beast or beggar; in the whole Nation, no other relic is left of the Discipline of Cartography." Jorge Luis Borges and Adolfo Bioy Casares, "On Exactitude in Science," in Fantastic Tales (New York: Herder and Herder, 1971), 23.

92. M. León-Portilla, as cited in Anthony F. Aveni, Empires of Time (New York: Basic Books, 1989), 185.

The cemetery of the Open City in the high ground was begun when two of the children of the founders died, one by fire and the other by water. The cemetery is located in a crevice in the plateau and is structured by a path that leads from its entry through the first two tombs to be built: through the tomb for the drowned child, which is a broken brick dome spiraling into the ground, then up a narrow path, which is more of a drawn line than a path, to the tomb of the burned child on the crest of the hill—a broken brick dome spiraling toward the sky. The lower tomb contains a stone seat built for a child. The path linking the entry and the two tombs divides the land into three areas that are allocated to the founders, the inhabitants of the Open City, and the relatives. There is also an open-air chapel and a cenotaph, which is a cut in the ground formed by two brick retaining walls held little more than two feet apart by steel rods. Beginning at the bottom of the crevice, the cut moves level into the inclined slope in a lightning bolt shape until, following it, one finds oneself surrounded by a tall room roofed by the sky. Powerful and remarkable in itself, it also evokes the apparition in one's memory of elements of classical mythology: of the labyrinth of Crete, of Dedalus and the Minotaur.

The Cenotaph

the mesoamerican sky in the sense that it is the ethos of the work and its initiator, philosophically, theoretically, and physically: in action. Instead of the analogical reading of natural phenomena as the sacred revealing itself, one finds the suggestion of reality, which includes natural phenomena, opened up to another dimension. Instead of priests as readers, interpreters, distributors of power, one finds initiators of the poetic activity. And among these initiators one clearly senses the strength of Godofredo Iommi and Alberto Cruz, who hold a shamanistic status not as distributors of power but, certainly, as seers and diviners and as those who self-consciously activated the field of activity.

The integration of space, time, and man through natural phenomena, in a semiotic system that includes poetry as both an element and an initiator, can be found within the work of the Catholic University of Valparaíso in almost every project of the travesías and of the Open City. Certain projects at the Open City, such as the Palace, the cemetery, the agoras, the Jardin de Bo, focus specifically on these relationships while others engage them from a more oblique position. The Jardin de Bo is of particular interest in that it weaves together natural phenomena and poetry in a physical space. It establishes key spatial alignments with the sun rising out of the land and setting along the timeline of the Pacific horizon. Yet, it also configures into the space of those alignments the rhythm and cadences of a poem of Ephraim Bo, joining the rhythms of nature as perceived in the horizontal pacing of the sun along the east and west horizons—natural time—with the long rhythms of the poem—the poem's time. The poetry becomes physical movement within the space in that one walks its rhythms, which are gauged to the physical paces of individuals in the stones and reliefs of the terrace. Concurrently, but at a different scale temporally, a different rhythm, the sun navigates the sky and horizon. Man and sun navigate the same space. The poem configures one movement as a counterpoint to the other. Poem, sky, man, and space intertwined by rhythms while the sound of the sea, of the wind, or of the rain breaking over the rough pavement add the tone. Space becomes music.

Within the native religions of the Americas, nature's structure is analogous to sacred structure, and concepts of space and time are the manifestations of this analogy. The theologian-historian Mircea Eliade defines the sacred: "The sacred is pre-eminently the *real,* at once power, efficacity, the source of life and fecundity. Religious man's desire to live *in the sacred* is in fact equivalent to his desire to take up his abode in objective real-

ity, not to let himself be paralyzed by the never-ceasing relativity of purely subjective experiences, to live in a real and effective world, and not in an illusion."[93] The sacred is equivalent to a reality that transcends subjective reality. And that which is sacred on earth is that which is capable of verifying the existence of another reality, of manifesting this reality, and of providing the connection into the realm of this reality. This implies that space is not homogeneous but interrupted by apertures into the sacred realm that generate either a hierarchical spatial structure or a dualistic spatial structure: a concept of space in which space is either sacred or profane, on or off. "For religious man, space is not homogeneous; he experiences interruptions, breaks in it; some parts of space are qualitatively different from the others. . . . We could say that the experience of sacred space makes possible the 'founding of the world': where the sacred manifests itself in space, *the real unveils itself,* the world comes into existence. The eruption of the sacred . . . affects a break in plane, that is, it opens communication between the cosmic planes and makes possible ontological passage from one mode of being to another."[94]

Spatial nonhomogeneity is not a matter of theoretical speculation but of a primary experience and attitude toward occupation of space and construction of form. The discovery of sacred space is more a recognition than a discovery, a naming rather than a finding, in that it is effectuated by signs provided by the sacred. And those signs are carried in natural phenomena: by comets, eclipses, droughts, floods, and other more gentle phenomena, all of which, though, are extraordinary in some way. Within the Native American religions, the world and all of its components are not merely natural in a romantic or sentimental sense, but instead, they are alive with messages that reveal the existential dimension of reality. "The cosmos as a whole is an organism at once *real, living,* and *sacred;* it simultaneously reveals the modalities of being and of sacrality."[95] It is a transparent world, a transparent nature in which the sacred is revealed through the tight space of the analogy.

Time, for the classical American societies, exists in a fixed and closed system. Repeating continually in cycles determined by celestial movement, sometimes simple, sometimes a complex overlay of phenomena—cogs of various sizes turning simultaneously as in the Mayan calendar. The repetitive cyclical calendars derive from and support mythological history and the belief that all things of creative importance exhausted themselves in the events that occurred at the beginning of mythological time when the world was constructed and defined. Within this concept of time, new acquisitions, revelations, and responses are always projected back to primordial time for their significance and meaning to be recognized and incorporated.

93. Mircea Eliade, trans. Willard R. Trask, The Sacred and the Profane (New York: Harcourt Brace Jovanovich 1959) 28.

94. Ibid., 20, 63.

95. Ibid., 117.

With modernity came history as a concept and relativity. The events of man and their significances become a product of history as modern man comes to see himself as a purely historical being, that is, a mutable product of history that is constantly changing and recreating itself anew, redefining our meaning in society and in our relationship to our physical and historical contexts. "Man opts out of the canon of authorized responses and finds that he is faced (both in art and science) with a world in a fluid state which requires corresponding creativity on his part."[96] Time no longer exists in a closed cyclical system but is continuous. Its movement is propelled forward along different trajectories instead of series after series of repetitive rotations. Time moves from the past to the present to the future, but it is the present that entranced the modern poets and surrealists because the present is the promise of the future and the result of the past. It can be projected both forward and backward. It is the pure essence of time, distilled to its smallest components in which its movement or passage still occurs, in which all the known and the possible overlap in the densest of spaces. The fascination with not only the present but, more important, the smallest irreducible increments of the present, the atom of time that, in a fluid and continuous medium, stands in for all of time—the "ultra-rapid delay"[97]—is what intrigued the surrealists and led to the generation of methodologies that thwarted the extension and prolongation of time in which the rational mind operates to obscure the pure experience (appearance) of reality with theories, hypotheses, analysis, classification, and so forth. Clearly this concept of time reduced in dimension, in thickness is part of the influence of the work of the Catholic University of Valparaíso, which is about working for the pure apparition of the real.

The atom of time that stands in for all of time is only possible in a concept of time that is continuous and fluid. Fluidity, as the easy exchange of one moment for another, in time implies a corresponding fluidity in space. The invention of a historical concept of time occurs concurrently with the creation of a concept of space that is continuous and homogeneous. For the modern French poets and surrealists, homogeneity is an important dimension of modern mental space that they embrace as part of the concept of the world in which the arbitrariness of a subjective position in time or space is irrelevant to the wholeness of the world. It is "a unitary vision of what is real, as opposed to the scission between the I and the world and the dispersion of the data of what is real in isolated spatial occurrences. . . . [Its work] is the material updating of the universe's space perceived as a whole, not atomized, the roots of which are present in the very conscience and constitutively form

96.   Umberto Eco, trans. Anna Cancogni, The Open Work (Cambridge, Mass.: Harvard University Press, 1989), 7.

97.   Marcel Duchamp's concept of a moment in time arrested or held on to (delayed) just long enough (ultra-rapid) to disassociate it from its conventional sequencing and causality.

In the work of Duchamp this kidnapped moment in time, this "delay," is simultaneously assigned form and stripped of its preconditioned value as determined by its relationship to ordinary causality. This work includes the "readymades," which Duchamp specifies as the "planning for a moment to come (on such and such a day,

date, minute), to inscribe a readymade.... The important thing is this clockwork character, this instantaneity.... It is a kind of rendezvous" with the "date, hour, minute, inscribed on the readymade as information," (notes for La mariée mise à nu par ses célibataires, même, La Boite Verte, Paris, 1939, as found in Marcel Du-

champ, Duchamp de Signe [Paris: Flammarion, 1994,] 49). The readymade belongs to a moment in time (not vice versa). It is the moment in time itself—when normal causality and value systems are completely thrown open to discussion and criticism—that is the operator, and it is the discussion and criticism part of its perception process. Thus perception and representation are identified in the artistic act, throwing into relief the unity of surroundings and the nucleus of the mind."[98] The wholeness of the world is not a static image but a fluid presence in which the subjective position is arbitrary and, therefore, irrelevant. Relevant is the nucleus of the mind, the imagination, which unmasks the wholeness of the world through the perception and discovery of correspondences in which meanings migrate from one site to another, across time and space. In the work of the modern French poets and surrealists, sites of mystery are disclosed in which these alchemical correspondences operate to release a sacred potentiality: the presence of the *real,* not the illusion provided by purely subjective experiences.

In the traditional sacred experience, space is not homogeneous: sacred sites are the presence of the gods (God) revealing themselves (himself), and the mundane is the field in which the transmundane is the exception. Within the modern experience, space is homogeneous, and sacred sites are discovered in the opening up of the transmundane *within* the mundane. In the former, existential meaning is prescribed, fixed and closed, a thing to be named, while in the latter it is a potential that moves and migrates, an open condition provided by the nucleus of the mind.

Stephane Mallarmé wrote "nommer un objet c'est supprimer les trois quarts de la jouissance du poème, qui est fait du bonheur de deviner peu à peu: le suggérer . . . voilà le rêve." (To name an object is to suppress three-fourths of the enjoyment of the poem, which is composed of the pleasure of guessing little by little: to suggest . . . there is the dream.)[99] Meaning that migrates between sites across space and time is dependent on semiotic openness. Instead of singular semantic and syntactic relationships in which the "naming" refers to that, and only that, which is being named, openness depends upon the way in which language is used to collect and disperse several or many images—the way in which the syntactic and semantic relationships between the elements of language, between words and phrases and even between syllables within words, are loosened so that meaning can attach itself at different points. The fact that phenomena are no longer tied to one another in a one-to-one correspondence prevents the fixing of a single sense at the beginning of the receptive process.

Once words are loosened from that which they name and from their semantic and even syntactic relationships, they gravitate to other sites, picking up meanings as they move, through the force of metaphor. Metaphor initiates the correspondences between things from which the modern poetic

engendered by the act that is the subject matter. The concept of the ultra-rapid delay is also at the foundation of Duchamp's work with "du hasard en conserve" (canned chance) —work such as the "3 Standard Stoppages" where "a straight horizontal thread one meter long falls from a height of one meter on to a horizontal

plane deforming as it pleases to give a new image of the unit of length" three times (Ibid., 50). In these works Duchamp amplifies the process, but a process that is extremely reduced in the temporal dimension in order to fuse, in the instant, "the idea of the aleatory and that of apparition, which are almost generic in his discourse as a

whole" (Gloria Moure in the catalogue for the exhibition, Duchamp, April-May 1984, Sala de Exposiciones de la Caja de Pensiones, Madrid, 176).

98.   Pere Gimferrer, The Roots of Miró (Barcelona: Ediciones Polígrafa, S.A., 1993), 24.

experience of the *real,* the transmundane, emerges. It is in the tension of the space of the metaphor that the modern experience operates.[100] In the pre-Hispanic American religions the sacred experience operates through the close static space of analogy. In the space of analogy, elements are overlaid on each other in a direct one-to-one correspondence so that one is lost inside of the other: the sun is a god; solar eclipse is the god's loss to man. In the space of metaphor, elements and their terms retain their distance. They remain intact as they are. The metaphor provides the gravitational force that links them. Through metaphoric operation—through the coupling of metaphors, or their transformation, or the nesting of metaphors inside of other metaphors, and so on—intentionally or intuitively, complex gravitational systems emerge in which each element remains in its own site with its own properties intact, but migrating from one semantic attraction to another. Migration, movement, is effected by the most remote of possible linkages, not through normal causality, in a universe where a different "physics" operates.

It is in this mental space that the work of the Catholic University of Valparaíso works, in the fluidity of modern mental space opened by metaphoric operation. Yet it also positions itself relative to the sacred space of the pre-Hispanic American cultures. The field in which it operates is the natural site of the Latin American continent and its semiotic relationship to a communal field of activity. But it engages this field through the fluidity of modern mental space and not the closed analogic mental space of the classical cultures in which the presence of the *real,* the sacred, is only the objectifying presence of the natural world.

The poetic activity of the work of the Catholic University of Valparaíso provokes the discovery of metaphoric correspondences in which semantic openness is the goal and often the result. Spatial phenomena are not attached to one another by singular relationships or hierarchical structure. Instead, one finds oneself in a multidimensional network of relationships, which requires a certain active participation in approaching the work. One becomes engaged within the creative aspect of the work even as an observer. Walking into the Music Pavilion in Ritoque, for example, a first perception emerges, changes, transforms in meaning. Leaving, another one appears, and in remembering, another. It began as an image of four windows placed in a hollow of sand to form a space. That space, once formed in the mind, began to interact with the site through poetry. It became a sounding box for the Pacific's voice and a filter for its light. It became a metaphor for the first instrument to be placed in the pavilion. But, once constructed, it is no

99.   *Stephane Mallarmé, as cited in Eco,* The Open Work.

100.   *Here the word metaphor must be qualified. It is used to signify not only the poetic device named metaphor but, more generically, to actually refer to any type of poetic—or spatial—operation in which the distance is maintained between the elements engaged by the force of the metaphor. (In* The Monkey Grammarian, *translated by Helen Lane [New York: Arcade Publishing, 1990] in exaggeration to make his point, Octavio Paz suggests that all language is metaphoric extension of the original primordial word since language itself is only inherently nonsilence and, therefore, it will always maintain a certain degree of distance from all other things.) The degree of the distance maintained between elements, or terms, clearly varies from the most remote of connections to the closest of correlations in which terms collapse into each other: analogy. Poetic operation, then, consists of metaphoric operation attached to rhythm and sound of language.*

longer an instrument only. It becomes a performer, a composer, a conductor, a window, a hole in the space, an instrument for reading atmospheric changes, a silent guest, just four windows inside a box. But its significance and its *presence* is precisely in the operation of its transformation, the *way* in which it can migrate from one site of meaning to another and the fact that it always carries with it the prominence of the sound and light of the sea, their blending—space as music—which is inextricably linked to its presence. And its significance lies not only in its presence but in its act of appearing, its apparition. Because in that act the metaphoric operation was set in movement, the first pull of gravity was conjured. In the Music Pavilion, as in much of the work of the Catholic University, nature is coupled to the conjuring, to the experience of discovery, to the opening up of mental sites of mystery where the experience of the world is potentially sacred.

Space being homogeneous, sites for work or construction are not sacred in and of themselves, not necessarily extraordinary in any way. It is precisely that in being ordinary, their meaning/significance—their presence—once provoked to appear through metaphoric operation, reverberates, through metaphoric operation, to open up other sites of meaning. Travesías throughout the continent and the concept of travesía applied to the Open City operate from this recognition. It is not the site that is important as much as the operation.

The Plaza José Vial Armstrong is the result of a travesía that occurred along the beach just north of Valparaíso in a place called Caleta Portales. Although located in a very mundane site adjacent to the public beach and a commercial fishing pier, it is a place that opens up the mundane to the transmundane and, importantly, includes the mundane in the transmundane; it includes the sunbathers, the vendors, the fisherman. Metaphorically, it is a city that serves as foreground to Valparaíso but also, as a space built to house a poem, it serves as preface. Through the juxtaposition of space, spatial metaphor, metaphor of form, plays in scale, and most important, the interplay of the inscribed poem—its light, its sound, its space—with the light, sound, and space of the physical site, an experience is created in which a mental site is opened up parallel to the physical site. Both sites are in movement, in process of becoming. Because the physical site is in a public space, it is not only the initiated who participate in the mental site or in the process of becoming; the uninitiated "visitors" are engaged in the creation as well. Not all, but some. And each of them, unintentionally, without wanting or needing it, finds his or her own reference points and mode of approach. But it is the

One of the stones of the Plaza José Vial Armstrong. "The air watches over my will, fallen from my hands into the void."

poem which serves as the point of entry into the work because words are part of everyone's process of communication whether the intended communication is poetic or mundane. Words belong to the mundane all around one as advertising, propaganda, or social notices. They are not foreign to public space in written form. In the Plaza José Vial, they serve to initiate, to begin. They serve to collapse the distancing between the mental experience and the visitor turned participant—a denial of the traditional threshold of sacred space.

Words initiate and, engaged in poetic activity, they continue to expand the mental site. "The air watches over my will fallen from my hands into the void." The words of the poem are inscribed into faceted basins within the stones of the plaza. These basins hold the sky as one's hands would hold rain or sea water. They are inclined toward the sky so that the sun traces shadows through the crevices of the letters. Words merge with shadowed faces, changing the sense and reconfiguring the relationships to the physical site and to the mental site. As night descends, the poem goes silent, leaving *its* shadow in the void. Its presence is an echo that transforms slightly with each reverberation.

⓫ *C'est des poètes, malgré tout, dans la suite des siècles, qu'il est possible de recevoir et permis d'attendre les impulsions susceptibles de replacer l'homme au cœur de l'univers, de l'abstraire une seconde de son aventure dissolvante ...* [101]

The Plaza José Vial is a space that achieves a sacred dimension in a primitive sense in that the metaphysical experience is not abstract. It does not rely on intellect as much as perception, and it is not abstracted from physical space, from the world. Instead it relies on the physical space and its phenomena to operate. "Primitive" religions specifically associated mankind's existence with the creation of the universe through cosmogonic myth, which was the story of the beginning of creation. Through the myth, an immediate relationship was set up between the structure of man's action on the earth and the structure of the universe as it manifests itself in the physical environment. This relationship was maintained through the myth by both the repetition of the story and the miniaturization of the structure of the cosmos on earth. Non-primitive religions that rely on divine revelation, as an intellectual epiphany, to understand the meaning of human existence, break this immediate relationship and abstract man's self-definition from an inclusive relationship with

101.   "It is from poets, in spite of everything over the centuries, that it is possible to receive and permitted to expect the impulses that may succeed in restoring man to the heart of the universe, extracting him from his debilitating adventure ..."

André Breton, les vases communicants, 170; English translation: Caws and Harris, 146.

the universe and physical site. The breaking of this immediate relationship with the universe means that we have come to rely on our intellect to understand the world and its reality. The tactility and sensuality of the religious experience and the world is lost.

Primitive religions and societies depended on the cosmogonic myth to transfer meaning and structure from the universe to man. The myth was an oral tradition. Dependence on the spoken word, the oracular, is an essential element of these societies, as it is an essential element within the work of the surrealist poets and within the work of the Catholic University of Valparaíso. The word is essential to man's thought process and, in the form of spoken mythology within primitive societies, it is capable of communicating "sacred history," which fuses human behavior, and social and cultural institutions to nature as a supernatural entity—that is, an entity that is a manifestation of sacred forces. Among primitive societies, knowledge of the myths is knowledge of the divine history of the world, knowledge of what the human heros did as well as the gods, and is therefore a paradigm for all human behavior. The cosmogonic myth, specifically, as a description of the creative powers of the gods and narration of the original creative events of the universe, represents the act of creation and, consequently, serves as the model for every kind of making: material and spiritual. It is through the oral tradition that this model and all mythology, along with the understanding and interpretation of their concepts and of the sacred meaning of the earth, is passed from generation to generation.

With the arrival of self-conscious thought and culture as an intellectual activity, the word was torn from its sacred service to mythological tradition and the existential meaning that man derived from the universe and from his natural site was lost to an abstraction of nature as landscape or commodity while religion became the abstract site of the metaphysical. From this point on, any emotional response to be derived from nature was subject to nostalgia, and with written word displacing the oracular, the spontaneous interpretation and permutation of communicated mythological meaning, effected by the oracle, is replaced by the bifurcation of meaning into fact or opinion.

In primitive societies, the emotional response derived from man's relationship to the world occurs through mythology, and it is a response that occurs in community through the participation in ritual. The significance of ritual lies in the fact that it is the representation and affirmation of the sacred relationship to the world made by the *community*. It is not a personal emo-

The founding architect, Alberto Cruz

tional response; it is communion. The initiation rituals, a body of rites and oral teachings intended to incorporate the individual into the social structure of the tribe, rely on producing an extreme emotional condition in which the novice is so psychologically altered that his or her existential condition is altered as well, enabling the initiate to be incorporated into the structure of the tribe and the structure of the supernatural. The individual's status as individual—his solitude—is broken to effect communion.

It is the rite that makes the mythic present through communal participation manifested primarily in dance, drama, and building. Structure at the physical level is integral with structure at the metaphysical level. Physical structure contains within it form inextricably attached to its cultural signification, which, in the case of primitive societies, is itself inextricably attached to the mythology relating man to nature through the divine. And it is accomplished through the oral word.

With the loss of myth defining man's sacred relationship to the world, the essential bond of man and his world, his physical site, was broken. At the Open City, the lost mythology relating man to his physical and mental site through the divine as transferred by the spoken word has been replaced with newly created "myth" that relates man to the nature and culture of Latin America through the poetic and is achieved by the word, spoken and written. The mythological base has been replaced by a poetic base in which language is not in service of the sacred story but of the discovery of the world and its metaphysical space. The poem *amereida* is analogous to the cosmogonic myths in that it narrates not only the genesis of Latin America but also describes the attitude of responsibility to that history, to the landscape, and to the essential poetic quality of mankind. However, it is not a story; it is a possibility of understanding, not the history of a beginning but the metamorphosis of a sensibility.

The word is restored to its status as nurturer, not of the mythological but of the poetic, and is what links the material work of the members of the Open City to the space of its physical and mental site through the poetic act, which operates as a kind of oracular rite. As an affirmation of the relationship of poetry to the creative act made by the community, it is the creative response that joins the subject and object of the rite. Like the primitive oracular rite, the speaking of words aloud is what merges the subject and the object in the activity and allows for the spontaneous interpretation and permutation of meaning. Unlike the primitive oracular rite, though, which is an *emotional* response solicited by the dissemination of the word, this is a *creative* response dependent upon the invoking of the imagination through the word.

The uniqueness of the work of the Catholic University of Valparaíso lies precisely in this activity in which there is communal participation in the creative process and in which this participation is undertaken through poetry and poetics. The participation is oracular in nature. The spoken word, engaged in poetic activity, is inserted into the pedagogical and creative process of the institute. The poetic rite is an act of communion striving toward sacred status. In that they both tend toward communion, the poetic experience and the religious experience are similar, as the Mexican poet and intellectual Octavio Paz elucidates in several of his essays: "Religion and poetry both tend toward communion; both begin in solitude and attempt, through the means of sacred nourishment, to break that solitude and return to man his innocence." In both, the experience of communion effects a change in state, and a recognition of that change in state, for those involved. The experience is similar, but modern poetry dispenses with divine authority and, even though it strives toward communion, it is always a dissident activity. "Whereas religion is profoundly conservative, sanctifying the social bond as it converts society into church, poetry breaks that bond as it consecrates an individual relation that is marginal to, if not opposed to, society. Poetry is always dissident. It needs neither theology nor clergy. It attempts neither to save man nor to build the city of God; its intent is to give us the terrestrial testimony of an experience. As an answer to the same questions and needs that religion satisfies, poetry seems to me to be a secret form—illegal, irregular—of religion."[102] While religion sanctifies the social bond, poetry, and especially the poetic activity that the surrealists engaged in, is a voice of dissidence. Communion within religion occurs relative to the word as it is used to interpret, explain, represent, or systematize the divine experience. Whereas in poetry, communion is through the poem in which language does not allude to, explain, recreate, or represent. It presents. It creates the presence of the *real*. In modern poetry the "sacred feast" is the poem, which creates the experience of the real. In surrealism, as within the poetic activity of the Catholic University of Valparaíso, the activity, not the poem itself, is the experience of communion—is the presence of the real.

In religion and poetry, the experience of the sacred is similar, and it springs from the same source. That source is *desire*. Profound desire to be other than what one seems to be, to be rejoined to a state of being that reason and consciousness hold at bay. At the risk of oversimplifying the mutable philosophical complexity of man's position toward reality, it could be said that at the inside of the relationship one always finds the opposition of the re-

102. Paz, "Poetry of Solitude and Poetry of Communion," 166.

lationship: man and world, man versus world; man as consciousness and the world as being. And, relative to this relationship, two polar attitudes emerge: one that Octavio Paz names the "warrior" attitude and another that could be characterized as the "mystic's" attitude. The warrior attitude toward this relationship tries to dominate, subjugate, and conquer reality through knowledge as power. "Like a warrior, man struggles to subdue nature and reality. His instinct for power is expressed not only in war, in politics, in technics but also in science and philosophy, in everything that has come to be called disinterested knowledge." This attitude requires the separation of man from his reality to study and analyze it and his relationship to it, from a superior position. This attitude, integrally attached to man's instinct for survival, tends toward a fracturing of reality into categories so that its information may be compartmentalized and managed by the appropriate science, discipline, or profession. However, this is not the only attitude that may be assumed with regard to reality and the world. The other attitude, the alternative to separation and domination, is immersion in reality through contemplation. "Contemplation may have no practical consequence, and thus one may derive no knowledge, opinion, no salvation or condemnation from it. This impractical, superfluous, and unserviceable contemplation is not directed toward learning, toward the possession of what is contemplated; it intends only to immerse itself in the object."[103] This is the attitude of the mystic, and it tends toward wholeness, unification. It recognizes the unity in all things.

Archaic religions held these two attitudes in tension. Domination-fragmentation and immersion-unity. Modern poetry operates in the same space of tension where thought and life—consciousness and being—are not separate compartments but "communicating vessels." Desire for life, being, is the source of the activity. This desire is what pulls thought—reason, consciousness—into the realm of being and establishes the tension. Desire, profound desire of being is the source of the sacred experience. In religion, it is desire as supplication, desire to communicate with the divine. In modern poetry, it is desire as conjuration to make present the *real*. And in surrealism, it is desire simply to conjure, to be in the presence of the *real* where there is no separation between opposing forces, and time collapses itself into that moment.

At the beginning of the endeavor, Godofredo Iommi said "La Universidad tiene que ser erótica, si no es erótica deja de ser universidad"— the university must be erotic. Eroticism is desire, the source of the sacred ex-

103.   Ibid., 164.

perience, but it is desire that transcends sexuality. It is a psychological phenomenon, a social and mystical phenomenon. It is a profound desire that is the substance of creation and the creative endeavor. It is the desire that allows one to suspend disbelief, to dismiss reason. "The sacred eludes us. When we try to lay hold upon it, we find that it has its origin in something pre-existent, something that is confused with our being. The same is true of love and poetry. The three experiences are something that is the very root of man."[104] Latent in all three is a desire to be complete again, not relative to one's position in space and time—to what came before or what will occur after—but pure being in which all collapses into the multiplicity of the moment, in which meaning is in the confluence of all opposites within the density of that space. That moment is the past and presentiment for the future, and it engages the homogeneity of space—the intimacy between things. It is this desire that is the substance of all great human endeavors and heroic undertakings. As Godofredo Iommi explained, Eros must be present in the creative act, in the passion that signifies the adventure of constructing life, in the eroticism that creation implies.

In the initial proposition of the Catholic University of Valparaíso to remove architecture from its doctrine, buried in mathematics and formalisms, and recenter it in the poetic word, is suggested an adoption of a critical rebalancing of the relationship between creative activity and the modern world. Creation requires a certain innocence, a suspension of disbelief, to occur. Poetry, as a revelation, returns to us that innocence, returns to us our "astonishment and fecundity."[105] In modern society the subjugation of reality through systems of knowledge, through the "warrior attitude," has destroyed the tension inherent in the opposition and alikeness of man and reality, the irreconcilable distance between and the intimacy shared. Knowledge and thought have been glorified while contemplation and the sacred dimension of being have been condemned to irrelevancy. Archaic religions held these in tension throughout the body of the society: the warrior and the mystic. At the moment when religion became dependent upon divine revelation, about conscious thought and, concurrently, societal division of labor created the profession of clergy, the tension loosened. Modern man further distances himself from the condition of being as he comes to deny the role of religion and sacred existence. Truly sensational discoveries in the sciences, knowledge systems, and technology along with their usefulness have successfully undermined the relevancy of the sacred dimension, and in doing so, the power that is at the foundation of creation. Desire—not for sex, money, or power

104. *Paz,* The Bow and the Lyre, *119.*

105. *Paz, "Poetry of Solitude and Poetry of Communion," 168.*

but for meaning—has been capped. The making of things becomes less than a creative act, it becomes part of scientific methodologies. It becomes analysis, transformation or translation, typology or critique, or synthesis: the replacement of two things with another, making both things different in the process. In modern poetry and, especially, the modern poetic activity of the surrealists, a fluid medium is assumed in which opposites and unlike things exist intact.

The novelty of the surrealists is in their discovery of ways of thinking, feeling, and acting, which attempted to connect pure presence, life and being, to thought. Thought and life are not separate but are instead communicating vessels. The nocturnal communicates with the diurnal. The novelty and relevancy of the surrealists lies in their vision of the world, which is absolutely inclusive. They did not deny modern scientific principles, tendencies, and discoveries but used them, thereby reintroducing the tension by which the world-universe is created. They did not deny science or technology because reality is inclusive, not exclusive. All things are connected no matter how transparent or obscure the connection. Marble stands in for sugar, love is connected to machines, and mechanics is connected to erotics. Nothing is what it seems: measurement, temperature, causality, physical phenomena, love. But of course it is the obscure that fascinates because it continues to cause wonder and astonishment as it reveals the connectedness in the most improbable and because within the wonder and astonishment is the revelation of the connection the mind has perceived, not through intellectual thought but through pure perception.

Surrealism is not so much a poetry but a poetics: a vision of the world in which the divine figure has been replaced by a poetic force that is powerful. This force is saturated with gratuitous and mysterious images, and it supports a vision of the world in which the poet is not a figure separate from the group but is anyone who attempts to challenge the force into relinquishing its images. It is a vision of the world that "brandishes inspiration like a sword" reuniting the mystic with the warrior.[106] It is not surprising that Breton and the surrealists were fascinated with the art and mythology of the Pueblo Indians, with voodoo ceremonies of possession, with masks, with magic and the occult. There is a fascination with things related to this union between power and the mystical aspects of primitive religions. At the same time, there is a rejection of the "religious" function of the artist and a rejection of traditional religion, which completely obliterated the immediate relationship between the known and the unknown through its rationalization of the mystique of the sacred.

106. *Paz*, The Bow and the Lyre, *154*.

The novelty of the work of the Catholic University of Valparaíso is in its commitment to modern poetry and poetics within the creative and pedagogic processes of architecture and, very specifically, in its commitment to the power of the word and language within these processes. Architecture is not poetry. Its medium is physical space and form, three-dimensional in nature. It is quantifiable and qualifiable and it is an incontrovertible citizen of the mundane. Its presence is of the world. Surrealism, as poetics not poetry, certainly implied its extension out of language into other creative realms. By engaging in poetic activity, the work of the Catholic University of Valparaíso allows itself through chance, mental and perceptual games, metaphoric operation, and so on, to discover its meaning and physical form, and to build and occupy this space: a space that has a gratuitous and mysterious quality and seems to refer to something on the other side of its physical reality. Through the employment and transformation of surrealist methodologies—the poetic acts, game playing, masks, travesía—the work is capable of reengaging through communal activity, through communion, a sacred dimension of existence in which the tension between thought and presence reappears to reestablish a certain elusive transparency between them and their world.

⑫ It is not insignificant that the commitment to modern poetry and to poetic activity is a commitment to the power of the poetic word and language, both written and spoken. Whereas normal speech tends to fragment and compartmentalize to make itself understood, poetic operation has the power to unify. Octavio Paz, speaking as the poet, presents the poetic operation as the creation of images, unified but open, through language. The image holds language in tension. It returns language to its original state of plurality of meaning while making present meaning of a unifying order: tension between meaning and nonmeaning, sense and nonsense.

•

Language is meaning: sense of this or that. . . . All communication systems live in the world of references and of relative meanings. Thus they constitute groups of signs endowed with a certain mobility. For example, in the case of numbers, a zero on the left is not the same as a zero on the right: numbers change their meaning according to their position. The same occurs with language but its range of mobility is much greater than that of other methods of signification and communication. Each word has a number of meanings which are more or less interrelated. Those meanings are ordered and made precise in accordance with the word's place in the sentence . . . of itself language is an infinite possibility of meanings; when it is actualized in a phrase, when it truly becomes language, that possibility is fixed in a single direction. In prose, the unity of the phrase is achieved by the sense, which is something like an arrow that forces all the words that compose it to aim at the same object or in the same direction. Now, the image *is a phrase in which the plurality of meanings does not disappear. The image receives and exalts all the values of the words, without excluding primary and secondary meanings.*[107]

•

But the image, consisting of several meanings, does not melt into sheer nonsense because at the same time that it is opening up *language* to the multiplicity of meaning, it is setting *itself* in the unity of the perception of itself. Any object we perceive, at the very moment of its perception, is a plurality of qualities, forms, sensations, and meanings unified, instantaneously, at that moment that constitutes the perception. This plurality of qualities is often extremely complex, even contradictory, yet we are capable of distilling them all into what we consider to be the object's meaning. This meaning is our relationship to the real, to reality, and it is the foundation of language. It is the acquisition of the object, of physical reality, through language. The poetic image does not fracture the experience of the real through analysis, description, scientific formula, or other descriptive methods that separate out its qualities, characteristics, and traits. Instead it recreates, evokes, resuscitates, awakens, relives the experience of the real by the way in which language is captured within the image.

"Every phrase has a reference to another, is susceptible to being explained by another. Thanks to the mobility of signs, words can be explained by words. . . . Every phrase means something that can be expressed or explained by another phrase. . . . On the contrary, the meaning of the *image* is the image itself: it can not be said with other words."[108] Or in a different order. Images cannot be reduced to an explanation or an interpretation because they have a direct link to reality through the way in which they are engaged by the mind.

The poetic image, the image provided by language, is very different from the images engaged in through the process of design related to the visual and spatial. Both are mental images. But the experience of reality, itself, for us is dominated by the visual field. The visual image is a translation of that reality already visually oriented. The poetic image removes the experience of reality from the visual realm, transfers it into the space of the mind through the symbols we have developed to name that reality—through language—and recreates that reality again. A different, but parallel, reality highly charged because of the tension that has been produced in the process.

107.   *This passage is quoted in its entirety precisely because it produces a visual image in which digits and arrows operate spatially to activate the image visually, as they do in the work of Paul Klee, Kandinsky, and many of the surrealist artists.*

108.   *Ibid., 91–95.*

Words engaged in the activity of poetic image making, operating parallel to or overlaid on visual image making, transfer this tension into the visual realm awakening the visual, and the physical, to their alchemical potentiality. Image replaces concept and imagination replaces conceptualization. Conceptualization fractures meaning and chooses from among the pieces while imagination unifies within the fluidity of the meaning.

The work of the Catholic University is an example of this: of the power of the word and language engaged in poetic activity to transform a pedagogic process and, more significantly, a process of making space where words activate the creative experience, provoking the imagination to join the illusive to the obvious, the ephemeral to the mundane, the irrational to the rational in a fluid medium. It is a creative process that is inclusive, embracing the complexity and plurality of its physical and cultural site through the transparency of modern mental space. A process that inherently recognizes the sacred dimension of space and, in a corollary manner, the sacredness of the natural world. And it is the creative process as a vision that is vigorous and aggressive. Testimony to this are the numerous constructions and projects found in Ritoque and strewn throughout the South American continent. These projects reveal their process of coming to be, their apparition, as they reveal their passion for the world, the desire for being of the world, which the process makes transparent.

For myself, the value of the work lies in its affirmation of the will to create, of the desire from which creation is constituted. The unity of opposites in the ability to suspend disbelief and enter into the void that is the creative act, the unknown—not the known or that which scientific and pragmatic methodologies can foresee. To let chance and the mind's own plenitude operate through its first mental tool: language.

I n d e x